Harpooning Donald Trump

A Novelist's Essays

Tom LeClair

*It is difficult to get the news from poems yet men die
miserably every day for lack of what is found there.*

William Carlos Williams

Published by MEDIACS
Mediacs@gmail.com

Also available as an eBook.

For Inga and Merrin

OTHER BOOKS BY TOM LECLAIR

Interviews

Anything Can Happen: Interviews with Contemporary American Novelists (conducted and edited with Larry McCaffery)

Criticism

In the Loop: Don DeLillo and the Systems Novel

The Art of Excess: Mastery in Contemporary American Fiction

What to Read (and Not)

Fiction

Passing Off

Well-Founded Fear

Passing On

The Liquidators

Passing Through

Lincoln's Billy

CONTENTS

INTRODUCTION

"I grow old…I grow old," J. Alfred Prufrock says at the end of his "Love Song," "I shall wear the bottoms of my trousers rolled." Since becoming a septuagenarian several years ago, I've chosen to roll up my sleeves, tell three lengthy stories about men facing imminent death, review three dozen books, and write essays about old writers still going strong and young writers going mostly nowhere. And yet, despite my recent activity, I was drawn to composing my "Final Words" as fictionist and critic. Then Donald Trump was elected, and I began writing words of political protest.

Those initial words were "RAGE TRUMPS HATE" on the first sign I carried in front of Trump Tower after the penthouse occupant's election. "Rage," not the "Love" I saw on other protest signs, was to me the unavoidable response and only recourse to the demagogue. Thinking back now, I realize that I was tutored early in rage by the literary — the masters and novels that influenced my criticism 40 years ago: William Gass, who told me in an interview "I write because I hate. A lot. Hard."; William Gaddis, who said his work arose from outrage; the mix of rage and comedy in novels such as Pynchon's *Gravity's Rainbow*, Heller's *Something Happened*, Gaddis's *JR*, and

Coover's *The Public Burning*, works I wrote about in a book called *The Art of Excess*. "Nothing succeeds like excess," I said in that study of large and large-minded "systems novels," and I believe it even more now when real news and fake news threaten any possible purchase literary fiction might have on the excesses abroad in Trumplandia. I'm no genius. No matter how outraged, I won't write one of those novels, but I have written these essays arguing and pleading for such a book — for many such books.

All but two of the essays here were written between Trump's election and his inauguration. *Saturday Night Live*, Twitter users, and sardonic pundits had been lampooning Trump for months. After he was elected, it was time to drive deeper under his thin skin, set a harpoon or two. I'm no crazed Ahab who would destroy his ship and crew for revenge on a "dumb brute." Actually, that sounds like Trump and the ship of state. But I know an angry white male when I see one. The barbed essays here will not reel in Moby Don, but I hope they encourage other litterateurs to use whatever tools are at hand to diminish his thrashing power over his credulous public. I'm pleased to see that in recent comments Paul Auster and Philip Roth share my disgust with Trump. Perhaps one of them will write the anti-Trump novel I won't.

In recent weeks, several journalists have called attention to dystopian or anti-Fascist literary works of the past. The most insightful and comprehensive of these essays is Sarah Churchwell's "'It Will Be Called Americanism'" in *The Guardian*. My essays treat less obvious or less explicit works that, I believe, provide more deep-rooted treatments of demagoguery. These essays were composed in a state of controlled rage, as I brought my street protest back to my keyboard, and later in a state of controlled hope when I identify those contemporary novelists with prodigious intelligence and outrageous imagination who might — who should? — contest the rule of Trump. Although the essays were written urgently, I'd like to think they are artful — stylish and entertaining and allusive — and therefore literary. The first three are personal — background of the novelist who became a protester, narratives of his protest at Trump Zero. Then the essays become more impersonal and interpretive as I discuss others' literary works, including a piece about novelists who I think are prime candidates for writing a profound and outraged literary response to the Trump future. Two of the essays were published by *The Daily Beast*, part of another was in *Full Stop*, and the piece on young novelists synthesizes recent reviews published in the *The Barnes and Noble Review*.

The first essay, "Final Words," describes the discouragement I have felt for some years about the efficacy of fiction and criticism, my own and others'. I wouldn't say I was enraged by the diminishment of "serious" fiction in the last couple of decades, but as a reviewer I have been dismayed and sometimes irritated by how many prize-winning novelists lack what Wallace Stevens called the "blessed rage for order":

> *The maker's rage to order words of the sea,*
> *Words of the fragrant portals, dimly-starred,*
> *And of ourselves and of our origins,*
> *In ghostlier demarcations, keener sounds.*

Trump's election got me out of my geriatric funk and out of my house. "Impressions of a Solitary Protester" describes my activities at Trump Tower in the weeks just after his election. "Turn Your Back On Trump" continues that story and proposes a way for individuals and groups to protest Trump's presidency without taking to the streets. "Trump's 'Age of Lead'" begins my commentary on possible models for literary response to Trump's administration. The essay opens with a discussion of Alexander Pope's great satire *The Dunciad*, where the phrase "Age of Lead" first appeared, and moves to lead in the water of Flint, to an attack on Trump's environmental appointees, and finally to speculation about which satiric novelists working now might write a Trumpciad. In a looping return to where I began as a critic, "The Public Burned" is an essay on Robert Coover's *The Public Burning* as a prescient forecast of the Trump circus and as an exemplary model for some future epic of excess. The next essay, "Donald Trump Won't Read This," analyzes Trump as the "pre-literate" man described by Walter Ong in *Orality and Literacy* and gives reasons for reading *The Iliad* as a cautionary tale about Trump's kind of oral "thinking." In each of these three essays, I name some contemporary novelists I most respect, not just because they might write about Trump but also because they are keeping serious fiction vigorous and, therefore, ready to respond to an administration threatening to do away with the National Endowment for the Arts and the National Endowment for the Humanities. "Systems Novelists We Need Now" discusses three of those novelists — Richard Powers, Tom McCarthy, and Joshua Cohen — who write the kind of "systems novels" that I believe are necessary to identify — as Coover does in *The Public Burning* — the historical and anthropological precedents of Trump's behavior and governance. The final essay treats *Moby-Dick* — the novel as harpoon — as a synthesis of the themes and forms discussed in all the previous essays. A brief "Epilogue" describes my occasional returns to Trump Tower and offers some new "Final Words."

Harpooning Donald Trump is in broad outline the personal story of an aged litterateur's unexpected rejuvenation by weeks of daily political protest. I tell it because I think my Prufrockian discouragement represents many other novelists' torpor, an increasing sense of our impotence or irrelevance in this century. The reasons are well known and need not be recited here. Until 11/9/16, we had no recent 9/11 to call us from our usual ways of making do, of making art. One of Trump's favorite words is "disaster." Now he is the disaster to which we need literary first responders. The story told here is mine, but I write to encourage others: Readers to find in literature of the past and, I hope, of the future the means of understanding and resisting Trump. Other literary critics to seek out and publicize work, possibly from fugitive presses, that engages current politics. Younger novelists to bring their intellectual rigor and artistic ingenuity to bear in big and weighty books that will harpoon small-minded and lightweight demagoguery.

If I may, like a Pynchon character, toot my own kazoo, what I think links these literary essays with the masterworks of late twentieth-century American fiction that I wrote about in *The Art of Excess* are historical perspective and systemic analysis. The older novelists — Pynchon, Gaddis, DeLillo — against whom I measure younger writers frequently include substantial histories that undergird their examinations of characters within anthropological, economic and technological systems. More recent novelists too often limit their horizon to the present and the family, to psychology and sociology — useful disciplines for an understanding of Trump the person but perhaps not adequately penetrating to understand Trump the phenomenon. I explain the origin and importance of systems analysis in "Systems Novelists We Need Now."

Although few words have truly final effects — divorce decrees, execution orders — I still believe that the literary deployment of written language can resist the empire of image and blurt over which Trump reigns. Of all the signs I wrote to display before Trump Tower, "DEAR SANTA: PLEASE TAKE TRUMP TO THE NORTH POLE" was the most frequently photographed. A modicum of wit got the passersby to take out their cell phones, and I directed their attention to a sign with more content hanging from my neck. Delight and instruct, as Horace said. "Impressions of a Solitary Protester" contains allusions to Satan, Socrates, Thoreau, Bartleby, and Whitman, a heady bunch of rebels to marshal against the whale. In "Turn Your Back On Trump," I hope my sport with the meanings of "back" trickles into the consciousness of anyone who opposes the backwardness of Trump. "Trump's 'Age of Lead'" rehearses the history of lead and plays with the metal as metaphor. In "The Public Burned" I try to mimic Coover's outrage and excess in *The Public Burning* to interest readers and other authors in that book's profound understanding of American politics as performance and display. "Donald Trump Won't Read This" opens with humorous reasons for not reading and ends with praise of Thersites, the lonely satirist in *The Iliad*, a work about the tragedy of the pre-literate, honor-obsessed mind we see persisting in Trump. Some of "The Only Book You'll Ever Need" is written in the second-person as I try to induce readers into the much resisted *Moby-Dick*. The harpooners in that novel all die, but the literary- and large-minded Ishmael survives to tell the tale, a model of intellectual pluralism that Trump attempts to destroy with his primary-school bluster.

In *The Public Burning*, Coover quotes Arthur Miller on the possibility of "lethal" art. Very few literary books have that final effect. The essays here are my modest literary contributions to what I trust will be — in the words of Gaddis's young, barely literate titan J R — a "groundswill" of other literary responses that identify the swill with which Trump has filled our ears and eyes.

FINAL WORDS

In 1972 at age 28 I wrote my "Final Words," a Ph.D. dissertation at Duke University. The title was part description, part joke. The dissertation was about death and comedy in then contemporary American fiction. The joke was that a dissertation is supposed to be "First Words" in a professional career. Since then I've published nine books and hundreds of stories, essays, reviews, and interviews. I still have at least half my wits about me and am not, as far as I know, terminally ill, and yet I feel like writing my final words. Maybe these will be them. If I thought my feeling was merely personal, I'd write the words, tuck them into my will, and go silent. But I think my desire is partly a response to current literary culture, quite different from the one I prepared to enter back in 1972. So for the possible instruction of the young — and almost everyone is younger than I am — I offer one individual's historical perspective on reading and writing books in two centuries. "Thoughts of a dry brain in a dry season," as Eliot says in "Gerontion."

Final words could be the last words in an argument, in my case about what contemporary fiction is important and should last, what fiction is trivial and transitory, the argument I made in *The Art of Excess* in 1989 that our systems-minded, encyclopedic, even "excessive" novels are our best books. Those last words are impossible because I see all around me that my argument is lost. Now, to quote Eliot again, "signs are taken for wonders," inchlings mistaken for giants such as last century's Pynchon and Gaddis and DeLillo. I know this kind of complaint is common from old men and old women, but I've been conducting an experiment on this matter for the last eight years, reading all the fiction finalists (and even all the long lists of ten introduced in 2013) for the National Book Award. In my judgment (and I was a judge in 2005), rarely do the most ambitious, largest-minded, profound, and ingenious books win, and quite often the few books of substance published in any given year don't make the final five or even the long lists. You can find my "data" and conclusions by Googling my name and National Book Awards, for I have published annual reviews of the finalists the last seven years in *The Barnes and Noble Review* and this year in *The Daily Beast*.

Several years ago I narrowed the issue by asking why we don't have in this century a Great New York novel such as Gaddis's *JR* or McElroy's *Women and Men* or DeLillo's *Underworld*. Garth Risk Hallberg's *City on Fire* has the necessary bulk, the artful excess and multiplicity of those earlier novels, but is limited by its essential conventionality. In that essay I adduced numerous cultural, technical and economic reasons why novels are not as adventurous and world-grasping now as they were 30 or 40 years ago. The rise of publishing conglomerates leads the list. But successful writers also bear some responsibility for giving in to what the age demands. My prime, sad exhibit is the difference between Pynchon's *Gravity's Rainbow* (1973) and his New York novel *Bleeding Edge* (2013). Even Thomas Pynchon surrenders to Mr. Softee entertainment. At least DeLillo resists: his *Zero K* is as risky and disturbingly grotesque as his early work. Though now 80, DeLillo shames the young MFA-holding writers who have received huge advances for large novels one expects to be consequentially literary but turn out to be what I've called "commercialit" in *The Daily Beast*.

Even if I had a bully pulpit like James Wood's or a hundred devoted epigones in LeClair's School of Excess, nothing would change reading habits exemplified for me by Amazon's lists of various books under 200 pages that can be easily skimmed on a phone. David Foster Wallace is dead and so is the heroic novel such as *Infinite Jest* and his unfinished *The Pale King*. Writers will go on producing modest and minor novels to please the small literary slice of the general audience. But mastery — the monumental mode represented by Pynchon and Gaddis and Wallace — appears done, so what profits a man, except for the freelancer fees, to continue lamenting like some Ancient Mariner that monsterpieces [sic] have been supplanted by artisanal consumables, that works one remembers for decades have been replaced by works that one forgets in a week? And if in this time of online "Comments" sections, Twitter and personal blogs, a Mariner should give negative or mixed reviews to novels by African Americans or women he may, like me, be called a racist or, as one literary tweeter said, "a huge dick overflowing with bad opinions."

Final words could also be a succinct summation, perhaps the name of a website. There's a computer game company called Failbetter Games. My site would be "Faillater." Failing as a critic, I turned to fiction late, publishing my first novel, *Passing Off*, when I was 52. Novels that followed — *Passing On* and *Passing Through* — measured no more than an inch apiece, but I was engaged in a Rabbit project with my hoopster narrator/protagonist Michael Keever. The "Passing" sequence, at about 800 pages, would be my serialized Big Book, not as long or wide as Updike's but at least an attempt to chart one working man's progress through recent history. Now, after some other novels, I've written the final words of the "Passing" series, *Passing Away*.

Because *Passing Away* is more insistently literary and Nabokov tricky than the earlier novels, I doubt that it will ever see print. The first three in the sequence were published by three different small, literary presses; two are defunct, the other has survived by switching to crime novels. Twenty years ago, the biggest and best independent presses would read the manuscript of *Passing Off* and even comment on it. Surveying current small presses, I found they are overwhelmed by manuscripts that large publishers say they can't sell. Some of these presses won't even look at non-agented manuscripts. Other presses make acceptance sound like the odds against winning the lottery, though you will have to wait a few years for your reward. With reduced support from the government and foundations, indie presses are like superannuated people struggling to survive. When I was middle-aged, I thought I could start small and write my way up and out to publication with larger presses that get their books noticed in the venues for which I was writing reviews, but just as I was trying to move up the conglomerates were cutting down on literary fiction. One encouraging fact for the young: a debut novel has a better chance of acceptance than a fourth novel by someone tainted by the small-press ghetto.

Final words could also be the curtain soliloquy. In Beckett's *Endgame*, the old chair-bound and story-telling Hamm says in his last speech, "Old endgame lost of old, play and lose and have done with losing." Hamm's last words are addressed to a handkerchief with which he covers his face: "Old stancher! You … remain." The handkerchief is his curtain and the veil of words behind which he hides himself. I realize that my complaint about small-ball novels and small-press publication may well be a rationalization for my inadequacies as reader and writer, but the discouraging effects of faint recognition, no matter its causes, are real. When the young Joseph Heller had his first manuscript rejected 22 times, so the legend goes, he kept plugging away. When my first basketball novel was repeatedly rejected, I kept sending it out. Fortunately, I had years to get my debut published. At 72, I don't have the same time or the same beginner's confidence in *Passing Away*.

Philip Roth announced his retirement from fiction with little explanation. I've found that words — even my main man Michael Keever's — come slower and harder, without the same kind of excitement present in my 50s and 60s. I have no patience with cinematic description, not much patience for commercial plot. I want only the characters to speak to one another and talk about each other. Maybe I should write a play. Only one of the three protagonists in *Passing Away* does anything dramatic; terminally ill, he arranges his own murder. His last words are to his brother, who is going shopping for him: buy "prune juice." I guess that's the much-remarked "late style" of minimal prose. In "The Last Days of Calvin Coolidge," the former president has uncharacteristic logorrhea because he is angry with wife and life. I had to invent his dying days to get words streaming from his purse-lipped mouth that one wag said looked as though he'd been born sucking on a pickle. Frederic Tudor in "The Emperor of Ice" is self-congratulatory and bombastic, an extreme, obsessed character I chose so lively words would issue forth. These two stories are in the "too late style" as the author, perhaps desperately, employs eccentricity and artifice to utter words that might satisfy Donald Barthelme's Snow White, "I wish there were some words in the world that were not the words I always hear!"

Final words could be an epitaph. The character who arranges his murder and asks for prune juice is Patrick Keever, brother of Michael Keever. Close to the end of Patrick's life, he personifies one of Michael's athletic saws: "love your luck." Patrick has been unlucky in love and in casinos, but still feels lucky to have been alive. He could have been, as Elkin's Franchiser says of himself, "a dot on a die." Michael admires Patrick's poor forked accommodation, and so do I. Patrick quits the game, "lost of old," on his own terms. A phlegmatic policeman with no need of verbal summation, he lets his last words be "prune juice." I'm not arranging my death, but I hope to arrange a few more last words than two. Influenced by my fellow point guard Keever, I'd like my epitaph to be "He Hit The Open Man." Updike's Rabbit was a shooter. Michael and I were passers, assist guys, not the stars but those who helped the stars by giving them passes. And I like the double meaning, too: that as a critic I "hit" the man or woman who left themselves open to punishment when they betrayed their art.

Badly educated in a one-room school, a father of one at sixteen, a laborer after high school, father of three when in graduate school, I love my later luck, my unlikely life as a university professor and writer of books. But now that I'm a pensioner I resist being a petitioner. Here is how old age comes up against the new age. Because editors of beleaguered book sections now try very hard to disseminate positive, happy talk, they ask reviewers to "pitch" themselves and books the reviewers think they will praise. Editors have taken over the diction of producers in the movie and TV business. To find publishers for fiction, writers are asked to pitch their marketing plan — describe how the manuscript fits the press, the book's audience, one's social media presence, the contacts who can furnish blurbs. Publishers' requirements for non-fiction projects have now migrated to art. I live in Brooklyn. I know it's only fair that I compete with the young scrabbling writers here, but, as Prufrock says about his undelivered romantic pitch, "would it have been worth it, after all"?

When I was seventeen, I was peeling pulp in the Vermont woods. It was a harsh job I couldn't refuse. With luck, I went from woodsman to "wordsman," and now I feel like refusing to be a pitchman. Saying "no mas" would not "disturb the universe"; it would just be a gesture I might remember with pride as my wits desert me. Opting out of self-promotion might preserve a modicum of dignity and throw some silent shade on a publishing world that has devolved, I believe, since I published my first review in the *Times* in 1976, years before some of my editors were born. I don't want to be frustrated and angry in my final years. If, as Hamm says, I decide to "speak no more about it … speak no more," I'd still read, perhaps older books I've missed. I'd still write emails to my friends. But I'd write no more about books. And write no more books.

Final words could also be the last words of an essay entitled "Final Words." Moving toward this last paragraph, I realized *Endgame* doesn't end when the lights come up. In the performances I've seen, the actors stay on stage while the audience exits. Hamm and Clov may want to end, but we're aware that they will be performing the same roles on that stage, saying their last soliloquies the next night and the next, waiting for the close of the play's run. Their continuation suggests a possibly happy non-ending for me. Words on the page have an attractive finality, but by writing these I have an odd sense of futurity. I could wait. That's the one-word reminder that Kafka is said to have posted above his desk. The final word of *Passing Away* is borrowed from Updike, the last word of *Rabbit at Rest*: "Enough." Depending on the tone, the word indicates one is satisfied or satiated. Maybe enough is not enough. Perhaps I've been identifying with the wrong Beckett play. There could be dignity, I thought, in waiting for a change or the end.

That's what and who I was — a man who had never publicly protested anything, a writer with little passion for writing — when Donald Trump was elected president. I had done nothing to oppose him except vote, but after the election I was enraged. Not just frustrated and angry, as I feared for my later years, but enraged. I couldn't sleep, I couldn't type. So I printed an enraged sign — "D.T.: REMEMBER HUEY LONG AND GEORGE WALLACE, DEMAGOGUES" — to take to Trump Tower in Manhattan. But before I left the house I realized the sign was the error of an old man who assumed the thousands of passersby would know who Long and Wallace were. I made another sign: "RAGE TRUMPS HATE," an alternative to all those "Love" signs other protesters, mostly young people, were carrying. My sign was just paradoxical enough to interest journalists, and I have been interviewed many times for television, radio, newspapers, and blogs, an experience I detail in the next essay. On the street, I get to explain why citizens must remain angry, resent fraudulence, resist the depredations to come, refuse to normalize the demagogue. I'm pretty sure my spoken words reach a much larger audience than my written criticism and fiction. And there are the numerous photographs of my signs that are posted on social media and might be read by more than hear my spoken words. In the future, I may write signs that are more literary. I like "MAKE AMERICA GRATE: ON WOMEN, MINORITIES, AND NON-CHRISTIANS." There opposite Trump Tower, I'd love to hoist high "BRING THE TOWERS LOW," an allusion to some of the final words in my favorite novel, *Gravity's Rainbow*:

> *There is a Hand to turn the time,*
> *Though thy Glass today be run,*
> *Till the Light that hath brought the Towers low*
> *Find the last poor Pret'rite one.*

But the three original words "RAGE TRUMPS HATE" are good. They are first, not final, words. They begin conversations. Answering questions about these words on Fifth Avenue, I'm still criticizing fiction, the false world according to Trump, and I'm still analyzing deceptions, as my novels do. But out on the street, with new higher stakes, I no longer feel, to quote "Gerontion" one last time, "A dull head among windy spaces."

IMPRESSIONS OF A
SOLITARY PROTESTER

The thousands who marched on Trump Tower in New York right after the election have returned to their hives and lives. Groups in the low double figures sometimes gather nearby at night. I'm the day shift, every day. It feels like the third shift because I'm usually a solitary watchman on Fifth Avenue across the street from the Tower. You can walk the sidewalk in front of the building if you agree to be searched by the police, but they would never let me stroll with my protest sign. You can also go into the Tower if you put your bag through an X-ray machine. I fold my sign into my bag and enter to use the Tower's underground marble toilet. Down there in the bowels of the ziggurat, I think of Trump way up in his penthouse and a line by the novelist William Gass: "I want to rise so high that when I shit I won't miss anybody."

Pedestrian movement several blocks in any direction from Ground Trump is curtailed and controlled by the waist-high barriers with metal bars you see at New York City parades. All the varieties of police swarm the area: Secret Service, a SWAT team outside the Tower's front doors, traffic police in yellow vests, community affairs police in bright blue jackets, regular officers with their low-slung duty belts, undercover cops (I assume), and what my contacts, the blue jackets, call the "white shirts," the lieutenants and inspectors. Many of the blue jackets in charge of pedestrians are women, Latino, or black, and some nod at my protest signs or even shake my hand when I arrive for duty. I think of them as secret sharers of the sidewalk. The white shirts are mostly white guys like me, and they don't like me protesting Trump on his block, their block.

There is a protesters' pen constructed of those metal barriers down the Avenue from the Tower. That's where the after-work groups of 10 or 20 are confined, shouting out their chants without disturbing those who live in the building. I reject the cage. I take my stand smack in front of what I heard one black cop call the "Black House" so passersby can take photos of my signs and the "TRUMP TOWER" sign behind and above me. I ask scores of smart phone users every day to post their photos online. Thousands walk past me in a day, and many may read my sign, but the solitary protester can now really multiply his semiotic impression through social media.

I'll stand at my post for some hours, and then a white shirt will come by and tell his blue jackets to move me. Once I conversed directly with a tidy whitey. He said, "You have to move." I said, "I'm not impeding pedestrian traffic." He said, "You have to move if you're on the sidewalk." I happened to be standing right at the curb, so I stepped back onto the street, where I was protected by a barrier from traffic. The officer walked off, took out his phone, and I got a visit from the blue jackets who told me to move because they really didn't want to arrest me.

Speech is free if you're in the cage or in motion. So I walk, as one blue jacket suggested, "like a turtle" up and down the block because I can't be arrested — I thought of the root meaning of "arrest" — if I keep moving. I stand still when people ask to photograph my sign, when I'm out of sight of the blue jackets, and when they go into one of their vans to get warm. But "going to and fro on the earth," as Satan tells God, doesn't give the same impression as standing firm, hands behind my back, sign hanging from my neck — posing as a lone "heroic" resister against the depredations to come. I'm not stopping any tanks, like that guy in Tiananmen Square, and I don't want to end up, like Bartleby, in prison, but being solitary is advantageous. One day a woman with a sign stood next to me, and the blues converged to explain that since protesters were now two — a veritable demonstration! — we had to go into the cage.

"RAGE TRUMPS HATE" got me interviews with print journalists from Canada, England, Argentina and France — and with TV channels in Russia, Japan, Sweden, and Kurdistan (whose reporter was amazed that an American knew who the Kurds were). Fox News and CNN are in the media pen right behind my post, but they never point their cameras my way. Like me, the lip-glossed and hair-fiddling talking heads want the Tower at their backs. With plenty of time to think, I imagine new visual memes: "Turn Your Back On Trump" or "Take Photo, Post Tower On Its Head." When the lights go on to illuminate the TV reporters, pedestrians stop to gawk at them and impede other pedestrians. That's when I realize police enforcement of the "stay in motion" rule is arbitrary and selective, for officers don't disperse the crowd of gawkers, valued New York tourists. But if three or four people stop at the same time to take photos of my sign, I'm told to move along by some among the blue jackets. They always cite "higher ups," and I wonder from just how high up the order descends. I like to think the petty occupant of the penthouse wants to cancel sidewalk mockery as he hopes to cancel *Saturday Night Live*.

Invariably, the interviewers' first question of me is not what I have against the outliar[sic]-elect but why I would be standing by myself holding a hand-lettered sign. I don't try to change anyone's mind. But if I'm sufficiently enraged to stand alone out in the cold every day, maybe I'll inspire my fellow citizens to stay angry. "NEW 3 R'S: RAGE, REJECT, RESIST." As another of my signs says, "NEVER SETTLE WITH THIS FRAUD." Since many visitors walk Fifth Avenue, I also address them: "TOURISTS: TRUMP TOWER IS NOT AMERICA. IT'S BABEL." I have some accompanying patter: "Free tour, Tower of Babel, coming down soon." I want visitors to take home or send home the impression that Trump and his tower of arrogance do not represent America. Of course, I know that's a lie like one of Trump's, for greed and hate such as his founded and expanded this land to the California gold Trump loves. But despite my country's distant and very recent past, I want foreign tourists to know America remains a republic of equal rights and free speech (as long as it's in motion).

Some passersby ask to be photographed with my sign and me. My data is anecdotal, but I'd say Canadians are per capita my chief huggers. Maybe no fences do make good neighbors. Europeans with their excellent English pat me on the back and extend their sympathies. On weekends, Latino parents want to photograph their children beneath my sign. To them I extend my apologies. Chinese tourists, of which there are many on Fifth Avenue, stop, puzzle out my signs ("GILD IVANKA, GELD DONALD") and ask permission before snapping. Maybe they think I will get in trouble if dissent is photographed. I suppose the security cameras overhead are recording all the activity, so some future anthropologist may modify my anecdotal data. And when facial recognition gets powerful enough, I can scan Facebook and other social media to check if my photographers have indeed posted my impression as they promised.

I don't get many insults, perhaps because my block on Fifth Avenue with its Prada and Tiffany attracts few visitors from the Benighted States of America. Although I know the passersby have little time to prepare a witty rejoinder to my signs, I'm still continually surprised at how dull the Trumpsters are. Maybe they're just being charitable when they offer advice: "Get a job" or "Get over it." I thank them and tell them that I have a job, protecting their First Amendment rights, and that "it" — the profiteering and hate — is just getting started. Some in "Make America Great Again" caps are curious. They ask, "How much you getting paid?" for they assume that a man Trump's age must be as gilt-ridden as he. Or they ask, "What country you from?" for they know no native-born American would insult a president, at least one not born in Kenya. Moderates plead, "Give him a chance." I refer them to Charles Blow's essay in *The New York Times* on the subject of "just get along" with the monster and show them one of my signs: "I GAVE TRUMP A CHANCE, AND HE GAVE US RACE-BAITERS AND IMMIGRANT HATERS." Then I tell polite pleaders that I may decide to give Trump another chance because I pity their populist loser of the popular vote.

Only once have I had to walk away from a rabid racist and once from a man who wanted Jesus to save me. No one has thrown anything except vulgarities at me, so maybe the generally pacific passersby should give me hope about "healing," which for some reason I hear as "heeling." But the Fifth Avenue demographic is probably not representative, for Manhattanites voted overwhelmingly for Clinton, and foreign visitors are not likely from the undereducated white underclass that flipped blue states to red. Someone told me I was just "picking at the scab," and if thin-skinned Donald came down for a few words I'm sure he'd say I was "picking on him," but I believe I'm "picking up on" a tradition of solitary gadflies such as the peripatetic Socrates and sauntering Henry David Thoreau. When Thoreau was in jail for refusing to pay a tax to finance the war against Mexico, Emerson came to visit and asked his protégé, "Henry, what are you doing in there?" Thoreau answered, "What are you doing out there?" When forced into the cage, I rattle the bars and ask the passing thousands what they're doing "out there," bustling along as if a demagogue had not blind-sided our democracy.

Maybe I should have called this essay "Confessions of a Solitary Protester" because I admit I'm traveling to Trump Tower every day partly to heal myself — cure my post-election dysphoria, work out my rage at Trump the shameless sham, rage at the racists who voted for him, rage at his first hate-mongering appointees. I'm already considering my Christmas message: "PEACE ON EARTH, PISS ON TRUMP, POX ON PENCE." A novelist who specializes in unreliable narrators, I was angry that Trump beggared my imagination with his extravagant inconsistencies and outright lies. All I could think about writing was signs. My first ideas were way too literary and allusive — "Rage, rage against the dying of our rights." "Never give in to Trumpelstiltskin." — so I made my debut with what I hope is not a flash fiction: "RAGE TRUMPS HATE." The fresh air has helped clear my head, and the experience of displaying signs has freed me to write these words that wouldn't fit on a piece of cardboard.

Shambling on Fifth Avenue, I'm anonymous, a man homeless in Trumplandia. I had wanted to remain anonymous, not because I fear our raging Lear or other social media trolls but to head off accusations that I protest for profit ("How much is Soros paying you?" I'm asked) or that I demonstrate to make an impression, to become a Big Apple celebrity like the Naked Cowboy, who prances by some days with "Trump" on his rump, or like Donald Trump the TV boss. But anonymity proved impossible. So I'll note that I've prepared for hoax-busting by criticizing fiction for 40 years and that I used to be a professor at a real university, not Trump's Fraud University that cost him 25 million dollars. Whatever millions I receive for these impressions, I, unlike the self-dealing philanthropist, will really donate — to the ACLU. (New sign, just realized: "DONALD'S CHARITY: TAKE FROM CHUMPS, KEEP FOR TRUMP," accompanied by sound effect of ringing Salvation Army bell.) I'd invite you to join me on Fifth Avenue, for I have a bag of signs that comment on Trump's bag of tricks, but then we'd be put in the cage. You could, though, stop by, say hello, and post a photo. As fellow Brooklynite and fellow traveler Walt Whitman says at the end of "Song of Myself":

> *Failing to fetch me at first keep encouraged*
> *Missing me one place search another,*
> *I stop somewhere waiting for you.*

TURN YOUR BACK ON TRUMP

Not long after I published "Impressions of a Solitary Protester" about my experience on Donald Trump's Fifth Avenue doorstep, the sidewalk dynamic began to change. Every once in a while, another protester would show up to keep me company for a couple of hours. There were Lindsey, who sang the first words of the preamble to the Constitution, and Jack, a young history teacher who carried a sign offering history lessons to Trump. Then one day I found myself standing in the middle of a loose line of five people selling pins, profiting like the huckster in chief from his election. Given the chill and Christmas shoppers' rush, my hand-lettered messages couldn't compete for attention with the vulgar images on the entrepreneurs' pins. "Dump Trump" pictured him as a pile of shit. "Impeach His Ass" Photoshopped his head on top of naked buttocks. Protest was being Trumpled, Trumpified.

Not wholly satisfied with my initial strategy — solicit photos of my various signs that would circulate on social media — I was trying in December to initiate a universal meme, focusing on one message that could be viral and vital, inspiring action. I wore a "TURN YOUR BACK ON TRUMP" sign on my back. Not turn your cheek or "Turn Your Cheeks," as I saw some mooning high school students do one day. And not turn away in defeat or in fear that your face will be recorded. But turn your back as New York City police did to Mayor de Blasio two years ago to protest what they considered his anti-police comments that, they believed, led to the murder of two patrolmen. That was a memorable gesture, scores of uniformed police turning their backs to power.

I asked sympathetic passersby to have their photos taken with me and my sign, our backs turned. Those who used Instagram promised to post the photos with the hashtag on the sign. But they didn't do it. I'm freezing my front and back for hours, and these cell phone "protesters" wouldn't take a few seconds to upload photos that could build toward a meme. Maybe the photographers feared being identified in some future surveillance state. Or perhaps the photographers were just at the Tower for entertainment, as the pin sellers were there to provide content-free amusement.

Profit and performance in the person of the Naked Cowboy came walking through most days, strumming his guitar, singing ditties insulting Obama and praising the Trump he had written on the back of his white briefs. He always drew a crowd I envied, but the TV cameras in the media pen never turned away from Trump Tower to tape him, not even when he copied his hero's attention-grasping vulgarity and called a newbie protester a "dyke." Perhaps frustrated, like Trump, at the media, the Cowboy sang, "Half the news/Controlled by Jews." At that, I got in his face, told him to "get the fuck out of here," and kept moving between him and the crowd as he tried to avoid me. His performance went on. The crowd laughed and clapped for the anti-Semite. The Cowboy would have certainly won a majority of these voters, released from "political correctness" by being in a crowd, an impromptu rally for ignorance and prejudice.

After the Electoral College voted, I wrote a new sign: "UNACCREDITED: TRUMP UNIVERSITY, ELECTORAL COLLEGE, RED STATE HIGH SCHOOLS." Emboldened by the College, Trump voters became more aggressive with the insults they tossed over their shoulders from a few safe yards beyond the citizen protester. Vulgarities turned into obscenities flying both ways. A man about my age, though thankfully smaller, had to be restrained by his wife when I refused to call Trump the President-elect. "Resident only, never a president," I insisted. I had been enraged by Clinton's losing the election. In front of Trump Tower, the winners were enraged that I refused to respect the loser of the popular vote.

With these experiences, some of my anger at Trump was redirected at people with whom I shared the sidewalk. Disgruntled with street protest but still believing in the potential of my backasswards meme, I deserted my post at the Tower for a while and came back to my keyboard to promote the meme. I discovered there was already a website with the same name as my Instagram hashtag: Turn Your Back On Trump. The site disseminates mocking images and quotes. I wanted physical action because the literal turning of one's back is a gesture of rejection and derision that denies the narcissist-elect exactly what he most desires — the gaze of others, the red eye of the TV camera. I hoped to watch attendees at the inauguration face away from Trump as he delivered the speech someone else wrote for him. I wanted to see marchers at the following day's women's demonstration walking with their backs turned, a special insult to the man who believes every woman wants to make the beast with two backs with him.

I believe the turned back has legs as a protest. Individuals can change their social media photographs, the backs of their heads registering solidarity. Alec Baldwin can incorporate the gag in his *Saturday Night Live* parodies. Recipients of Academy Awards will reach behind their back to grab the Oscar. City councils, sports teams, and other small groups could be photographed from behind. American imagination will reign, a crowd of backs will rein in Trump. Christo can assemble thousands of people to encircle Trump Tower in a chain chanting "Take America Back."

The meme has resonance because it rejects Trump's promise to take America backwards to a coal-burning and cross-burning time, back to the state of his own infantile emotions and primary-school ignorance. Some of his cabinet appointees favor turning their agencies into backwaters or Blackwaters. Democrats in Congress and forward-looking progressives in the media must face down these challenges to the republic. Those of us figuratively out in the cold can encourage our representatives by using our creativity to engage in this gesture of refusal whenever and however we can.

On social media, it will be easy to Photoshop backs and mock Trump and his strumpets. But I think "Turn Your Back" can alter language out in the world. Those who reject Trump and his policies can band together as "Backers." I envision a group called "Backers Against Hackers" to press Congress for a full investigation of the Russian cyberattack that helped elect Trump. Bumper stickers — "Get Off My Back" — can be repurposed. "Backing into" a success would no longer have a negative connotation. "Never back down" will have a new meaning. So will "back against the wall," Trump's wall. Though severely limited linguistically, Trump made his name a brand, a word with new associations, a meme. Opposition needs a counter word, and I suggest "back" is it. Get back. Back off. Fight back. All will have the association of Christ's words to Peter — "Get thee behind me Satan" — that accuse Peter of too much interest in "the things of men," in earthly power.

My back to the future movement may never go viral, but I still have faith in the stealth power of words. Now that you've read this essay, I believe that every time you see Trump scratch the backs of his donors you will think of "Turn Your Back" and imagine ways to resist the corruption to come. I was with her. Now I'm with Charles M. Blow of *The New York Times* who has eloquently and persistently articulated the rage citizens must retain to prevent Trumplandia's further back-sliding from American principles and ideals. To be brief and to honor the courageous Mr. Blow, we can call that rage "Blowback."

TRUMP'S "AGE OF LEAD"

Three-hundred years ago, the British poet Alexander Pope published a mock-epic poem entitled *The Dunciad* in which he "hailed" a "new Saturnian age of Lead." Dedicated to Jonathan Swift, Pope's poem satirized the dunces of his time ruled by the Queen of "Dulness," who sounds like Donald Trump in drag:

> *She, tinsel'd o'er in robes of varying hues,*
> *With self-applause her wild creation views;*
> *Sees momentary monsters rise and fall,*
> *And with her own fools-colours gilds them all.*

In different editions of the poem, the Queen selects two dumb men of little talent to be her consorts. Pope names the dunder-headed political figures who gather round the rulers, and he identifies hack writers who serve as surrogates by writing propaganda pamphlets and poems on demand. As a Catholic, Pope could not wholly align himself with either of the two primary parties of his time, so he directed his rage at individual dullards who lusted for power and the Grub Street scribblers who promoted them. Pope was relentless, writing hundreds of rhyming couplets, sometimes skewering the hapless with wit, at other times slashing them with insult.

Some years after the first edition, Pope added a fourth "Book," more outraged and pessimistic than the first three. Here the second King of Dulness, one Colley Cibber, also known as "Bayes," is described as if he were a victim of lead poisoning:

> *Swearing and supperless the hero sate,*
> *Blasphemed his gods the dice, and damn'd his fate;*
> *Then gnaw'd his pen, then dash'd it on the ground*
> *Sinking from thought to thought, a vast profound!*
> *Plunged for his sense, but found no bottom there,*
> *Yet wrote and flounder'd on in mere despair.*
> *Round him much Embryo, much Abortion lay,*
> *Much future Ode, and abdicated Play;*
> *Nonsense precipitate, like running lead,*
> *That slipp'd thro' cracks and zigzags of the head.*

In his prose "argument" preceding Book IV, Pope summarizes its action: "the Goddess coming in her majesty to destroy Order and Science, and to substitute the Kingdom of the Dull upon earth: how she leads captive the Sciences, and silences the Muses; and what they be who succeed in their stead. All her children, by a wonderful attraction, are drawn about her; and bear along with them divers others, who promote her empire by connivance, weak resistance, or discouragement of Arts." The "Kingdom of the Dull," an excellent description of the minds Trump gathers around him to speak for this inarticulate and vulgar "king."

A self-educated Classicist, Pope knew history and the ancient Greeks' ideas about the devolving Ages of Man: from Gold and Silver to Bronze and Iron. And as an eighteenth-century empiricist, Pope had some idea that lead was a toxin, a cause of Dullness. Facing the "Nonsense precipitate" of a Trump presidency, the United States of America needs an author with the daring passion of Pope, a writer who will bring history and science, art and rage, entertainment and instruction, to bear on an administration of energetic Dullness. The mock epic has long since disappeared as a form, but the mocking novel is still with us, though one of its greatest practitioners, William Gaddis, has departed. "Topicality," the Creative Writing teachers warn in their tenured seminar rooms, "is an aesthetic sink hole." But *The Dunciad* is still taught, Dante's *Inferno* still read, Aristophanes' plays still performed — and all include the authors' enemies lists. Some years ago, a profile in *The New Yorker* celebrated "Dangerous Don DeLillo," but his political intervention was in the past, the Kennedy assassination in *Libra*. We need a dangerous writer of the present, of the near future, a person who knows the facts and players, as Pope did, a person who can incorporate contemporary fools into a massive satire, like Pope's, of Dangerous Dullards.

If lead was primarily a metaphor for Pope, it's news now. It shouldn't be. Since the beginnings of western civilization, lead has been dangerous — and not just in bullets or in the alchemical experiments that affected Newton's sanity. Lead in the water of the Roman aqueducts may have been a cause of the fall of the Roman Empire, though lead in the Romans' pewter goblets and wine probably had more effect on the rulers. Could the Romans have known better? They had the example of ancient Egyptians who used lead to deleterious effect in their cosmetics. The Egyptians might have learned from the inhabitants of Sumerian Ur, where lead was first used, making lead the ur-element.

Those were early times. Science was limited. Last century we knew better, taking the lead out of gasoline and pesticides, removing lead from paint. But something about lead makes people dumb. We were too dumb to replace the lead pipes installed a century before. Officials in Flint had the measuring devices to monitor the water moving through those pipes, but it was easier not to. Or cheaper.

In Classical Greece money was made of — and from — lead. One source of the wealth of Athens was the lead mines of Lavrion down the coast of Attica. Until recently, one could see hillocks of lead slag around the harbor. Running water through lead pipes in Flint seems to have been a matter of economy, unless you know that "economy" comes from Greek, where it meant "home management."

I discovered the long sorry history of lead — or humans' use of lead — when researching my "Museum of Lead" in a novel called *The Liquidators*. One contemporary character, a plumber, died of lead poisoning. His son designed the Museum to demonstrate that humans have been liquidating themselves for more than five thousand years with the mineral that was most easily liquefied. I'm not saying that the Governor or other officials in the state of Michigan should have read *The Liquidators* and heeded its warning. My Museum was just a thumbnail history of dumbness that anyone charged with the health of citizens could and should have known.

All this is now obvious about lead itself. It has a long half-life. Perhaps its second half will again be as a metaphor, as it was for Pope. Lead has for centuries been associated with weight. I prefer its malleability. Since the Renaissance, western civilization has had an alchemical obsession, turning lead and every other substance into the gold Trump loves — into profit — with ever more sophisticated methods of making nature, including atoms, malleable — transformable, usable, and salable. The result is hundreds of years of substance abuse. Perhaps the most far-reaching industrial alchemy was putting lead into gasoline so we could move bodies faster. Then we had lead in our computers to move information faster. But as the narrator of *The Liquidators* says, "lead leaches." From mines to minds, from metal to metaphor. Everywhere we read now that humans must be malleable, willing to be formed by new circumstances, willing to change jobs throughout their lifetimes, just as malleable politicians such as Trump and his strumpets are willing to deny the facts in their face to achieve power and profit. Anything substantial, any solid principle, can be liquidated. That, to me, is the lesson of lead in Flint, a lesson writ large in the Trump presidential campaign and his forthcoming administration.

In a city named for a very hard stone, Flint officials were malleable or claimed the scientific evidence about lead was or calculated the poor citizens of the city were. Lead is used as a shield, in the apron you wear at your dentist's, in atomic reactors. But now that lead is in the bodies of Flint residents, I doubt officials can shield themselves with the excuse that "we were dumb." From what I've read, the Governor and other officials were not drinking that lead-laced water. And Donald Trump high in his tower drinking imported bottled water: what is his excuse for dim ignorance?

Lead lasts. It can be removed from the body by a process called chelation. But that is complicated and can have dangerous side effects. You can't reverse widespread lead poisoning by putting some other element into the water supply. Ancient Greeks told the future by the way small drops of lead congealed in water. The future effects of lead in Flint, especially on the brains of children, are difficult to measure. In "The Alchemist," Brueghel — more than 400 years ago — seemed to recognize the danger to children who are pictured trying to escape the lead fumes. Some scientific studies associate early lead poisoning with later criminal behavior. Let's hope Flint's children don't grow up to be as criminal as the adults who poisoned them, adults now being belatedly prosecuted.

The election of Donald Trump brings the possibility of a United States of Flint, polluted from sea to leaden sea. Like lead-headed generations before him, he and his climate deniers embrace — or pretend to embrace —

ignorance of science and history. Trump played dumb and played to ill-educated voters to pursue power and profit at the expense of public health. He posed as the Alchemist-in-Chief who could turn base matter, as well as base motives, into gold or, more precisely, gilt. He promised to "Make America Great Again," as it was before lead was removed from gasoline in 1996, even before the Environmental Protection Agency was founded in 1970. He was fond of calling his rivals "disasters," characteristic hyperbole ignorant of the root and usual meaning of the word: an ill-starred event of large proportion. Given Trump's appointees to positions responsible for the environment, "disaster" could well be the right word in the future.

Trump's nominee for the E.P.A., Scott Pruitt, has long been in bed with the producers of fossil fuels in his home state of Oklahoma and is a whore of the first order, a holocaust denier — the gradual but accelerating holocaust of global warming. Under Pruitt, the letters E.P.A. will stand for a new name: the Environmental Pollution Agency. When asked in his confirmation hearing about lead, Pruitt, according to *The New York Times*, "acknowledged a lack of familiarity with lead poisoning." The politicians of Flint are now required to make bottled water available to citizens. How will Pruitt manage the canned air that will be necessary when he gets through with the nation's atmosphere?

For the Energy Department, Trump nominates another candidate from an oil-producing state, Rick Perry of Texas who wanted to do away with Energy, as well as the E.P.A., presumably because the environmental regulations of recent administrations have limited the pollution (and profits) of extractive industries. Like Pruitt, Perry is a climate change denier who, as governor, made sure references to climate were scrubbed from state documents. Since Trump promised miners to bring back coal, his

Energy secretary will no doubt prostitute himself for coal-burning energy. When, in his confirmation hearing, Perry admitted that he accepted the job without knowing that it entailed protecting America's nuclear arsenal, I wondered if he'd been drinking Flint water or Trump's Kool-Aid.

Not content with a Flint America, Trump goes global and proposes to fill out his Team Pollution with Rex Tillerson for Secretary of State. As the Attorney General of Oklahoma, Pruitt had to limit the profits he could accrue from his oil and gas associations. As the head of Exxon, a multinational with a gross income larger than some medium-size countries, Tillerson has reaped millions from his corporation's contributions to climate change. Though Exxon in its advertising accepts the science of climate change, the corporation still funds groups opposed to the science and spends millions more on lobbying than on renewable energy. As a friend of Putin, Tillerson will support opening new oil fields constrained by sanctions against Russia. With Tillerson as Secretary of State, Coolidge's statement that "the business of America is business" will be shamefully true.

The residents of Flint did not know what was coursing through their pipes and blood. Trump called global warming a hoax perpetrated by China. He and his three Fossil Fools will attempt to hoax the American public into ignorance about pollution and climate change, just as the petroleum industry covered up for decades information about the poison Americans were breathing because of leaded gas. The governmental administrators of Flint were eventually caught lead-handed. They were low-level mafiosos. The dons controlling the United States of Flint will be more difficult to bring to justice because, of course, the Department of Justice will also be headed by a man, like the Fools, who hopes to see his department's power to protect Americans diminished.

"Poems make nothing happen," W. H. Auden famously said. But novels have — *Uncle Tom's Cabin*, *The Jungle*, *Grapes of Wrath*, *Catch-22*. I can think of no equivalent fiction published in this century, but there must be young writers who will be sufficiently enraged by Trump to write a Trumpciad. The day after the inauguration, Michael Moore said the thin-skinned Trump "could be the first president taken down by satire." Unfortunately, the author of *A Confederacy of Dunces*, John Kennedy Toole, died young. In a recent interview with *The Guardian*, my Brooklyn neighbor Paul Auster said he was "appalled" and "tormented" by Trump's election, but Auster isn't a natural satirist. Russian-born Gary Shteyngart used to write barbed political satire before he became an entertainer. Ben Fountain's *Billy Lynn's Long Halftime Walk* ferociously satirized the patriotic show put on by "America's Team," the Dallas Cowboys. Joshua Ferris's three novels have become increasingly absurdist in their representations of American life. Rachel Kushner, author of *The Flamethrowers*, has the political interests and seems to have the anger to write the Trumpciad. Maybe the DeLillo-influenced Dana Spiotta, whose novels analyze monsters of the media, will step up. But if it's savage satire that we want, Paul Beatty, author of the Booker-winning *The Sellout*, is our man. Any African-American who will risk writing a novel about a black man who reinstitutes slavery will certainly have the courage to compose a Trumpciad for our new Age of Lead.

THE PUBLIC BURNED

Donald Trump hasn't even been inaugurated, but I am already impatient for some quick and angry fiction writer to publish a novel dealing with the Artist of the Deal. Writing before the election, the veteran political novelist Thomas Mallon outlined in *The New Yorker* what he would do in a novel about the campaign, but said he was too disgusted to write it. Surely rage will move others with stronger stomachs to engage the ugly campaign and the possibly uglier administration filled with spiteful know-nothings and canny profiteers.

While we await what I called the Trumpciad in the previous essay, we are fortunate to have Robert Coover's *The Public Burning*, an encyclopedic novel published in 1977 that quotes Pope: "Aghast I stood [before] a monument of woe." I've been writing about American fiction since the late 60's, and I think that no novel gives us better understanding of Trump's election than *The Public Burning*. Coover knows rage. In 2014, he published a thousand-page sequel, *The Brunist Day of Wrath*, to his first novel, *Origin of the Brunists*. A wrathful Public Burning II would be welcome, but the original took him many years to write, the Brunist sequel came 48 years after *Origin*, and he is 84. So today it's back to 1953 and the public electrocution, in Coover's imagination, of the "atomic spies" Ethel and

Julius Rosenberg in Times Square, the "Entertainment Capital of America," in a saturnalia directed by the flitting Superhero and Barnum and Bailey ringmaster Uncle Sam.

More complimentary than anything I can say to recommend *The Public Burning* are facts surrounding its publication. Coover's initial publisher refused to release the novel for fear of libel. Another publisher attempted to emasculate it. Originally intended for the Bicentennial, publication was delayed for a year by the press that did bring it out. Many of the reviews were rabidly negative as critics, who had not yet experienced the offenses of Trump, were grievously offended by Coover's presentation of the Rosenbergs as witch-hunt victims, Vice President Nixon as a sniveling careerist, Uncle Sam as an imperialistic sodomist, and by the novel's formal and stylistic innovations. Structured as a three-ring circus, *The Public Burning* perfectly represented what the Russian critic Mikhail Bakhtin called the "carnivalesque," a radically subversive style of excess and satire that Bakhtin traced back to the Feast of Fools. If paper-skinned Donald Trump thought the cast of *Hamilton* had insulted Vice-President-elect Pence, the Executive Tweeter would have been apoplectic at how Coover mocks Vice-President Nixon. And if the paranoid Trump who attacks tame sketches on *Saturday Night Live* had been one of the fools in *The Public Burning*, he would have launched teams of legal drones at Coover and his publisher — and would have used the novel as evidence to support his desire to strengthen libel laws and weaken free speech.

The Public Burning intentionally violates traditional fiction's canons of good taste, but it is an exceptionally artful historical novel. The private and public lives of the Rosenbergs and Nixon have been scrupulously researched, and minor political characters have been swooped from the newspapers and public records of the time. Knowing that reviewers and other readers would take issue with his imaginative transformation of the Rosenbergs' execution, Coover takes great pains to make the realism of his magic realism unimpeachable — documentary and super-realistic. Even his magic — the figure of Uncle Sam — is a compendium of American history and discourse. Coover has said he wanted the novel "to seem to have been written by the whole nation through all of its history," and braggart Uncle Sam spouts lines from an amazing variety of popular culture sources. Because of its encyclopedic range and its shifting points of view, prose chapters and poetic interludes, *The Public Burning* may at first seem as chaotic as a crowd out of control, burning with murderous passion, but the novel is in fact carefully ordered, just as a three-ring circus is. Patterns of character doubling and skeins of metaphor emerge from the welter. Comedy and tragedy merge as the plot narrows to the absurd. All this is to say that *The Public Burning* will reward the literary reader in its own right, independent of how it seems to forecast and reveal the world of Donald Trump.

Coover studied anthropology in college, and it is the influence of that discipline that enables him to dig beneath psychology, sociology, economics and conventional political theory to see the deep structure of political life in America. In *Negara*, Clifford Geeertz's study of nineteenth-century Balinese culture, he found — I'm simplifying here — that the authority and power of rulers came from performance, from display, the grander the better, rather than from Western notions of command and force. Geertz called Balinese politics the "theater state." Coover brings this interpretation to the politics of the 1950s. Politics has always been at least partly about performance, the candidate's appeals to the crowd, but Coover recognized that, as he has Nixon say, "This is a generation that wants to be entertained." Personal ethics, policies, laws, codes of behavior, performance of duties — all are sacrificed to entertainment in Coover's America decades before reality TV and Internet cat videos.

Nixon is the realistic version of the performer, the clown in Coover's circus, capable of both bathetic appeals to others and amusing pratfalls for others. In 2017, Coover's portrait of a much studied Nixon will not be news, but the novel's presentation of the self-made (for others) man is remarkable for how Coover connects psychological detail to sociological — and anthropological — dynamics. Nixon is one version of democratic man, "free" from the constraint of some inherited, intrinsic identity. Feeling nothing himself, Nixon desperately solicits the approval, respect, and applause of others, a performative or extrinsic identity. He is tricky, pompous, self-serving and self-pitying, always aware of the "audience" even when alone.

Nixon the politician for life is Donald Trump the attention-mad New York developer who leveraged himself up from tabloid entertainment and guest of Howard Stern to business failure and conspiracy theorist to successful showman and hate-mongering political candidate. In his early years, Trump was willing to play the clown to garner publicity as he plastered his name all over grandiose buildings. When I am protesting in front of Trump Tower, I tell obvious Trump supporters that it isn't really The Tower. "Wail, what is it then?" "A façade," I tell them, "like the man." We know all this about Trump now, may have known it for a few decades when he was not taken seriously. What Coover recognized was that performance was deeply ingrained in American culture 70 years ago, long before what we now know as the Entertainment State and before an entertainer could reach his audience 24 hours a day with his Twitter account. Coover's Nixon attempts to escape his role as clown, but makes a greater fool of himself by adopting a movie-inspired role for which he is unsuited: heroic rescuer of the damsel in distress, Ethel Rosenberg. Though humiliated in Times Square, as Trump was at a roast by Obama for the developer's "birther" campaign, Nixon the needy no-man is ultimately accepted by Uncle Sam as a future president. It's the Trump success story, one that relied on Nixonian strategies in the campaign.

The national and global politics presented in *The Public Burning* are religion-rooted, Manichean (the American Children of Light versus the Communist Forces of Darkness), and paranoid, Americans fearful of atomic attack by the Russians to whom the Rosenbergs were convicted of passing secrets. As if to fit into this part of the essay, Trump tweeted not long ago that a new nuclear arms race is in order because he feared America was falling behind the Russians. Uncle Sam, as personification of American imperial power, instructs Nixon in the political uses of fear and in the pragmatics of scapegoating. The Jewish and New York City dwelling Rosenbergs fit the role of sacrificial victims just as immigrants and Muslims and cosmopolitan "elites" fit the role of scapegoats for Trump as he campaigned in the "heartland," the "real" America of undereducated white Christians. For Coover, the appeal of performance in America is so strong that the Rosenbergs seem to accept their role. Once convicted, they give up human particularities to become abstract symbols of injustice. Americans and others identified by Trump as enemies of the homeland could try to resist the role he foisted upon them, but he controlled the space of performance — the visual media, the theater state — where power is asserted, repeated, maintained. Like good liberals, the Rosenbergs respected legal codes and expected the courts to protect them, but the courts were no competition for the hysteria whipped up by Uncle Sam for the entertainment and instruction of the American people who, Coover implies, wanted a ritual sacrifice of the kind performed by "primitive" cultures to protect themselves from nature and the gods. Regression and atavism rule Coover's world, just as they did Trump's "Make America Great Again" rallies.

It's in the "god" of *The Public Burning*, Uncle Sam, that Coover most strikingly foresees Trump and his public. Based partly on Sam Slick, the Yankee peddler, Uncle Sam pretends to be a populist strong man defending American Christianity and protecting the little people from domestic and foreign evil, but in fact Sam is an "incorrigible huckster, a sweet-talking con artist," a protean shape-shifter, the impure principle of performance and entertainment, controlling characters and events to perpetuate his power to control characters and events. It is Sam who moves the execution from the prison at Sing Sing to Times Square where he assembles entertainers, officials, and celebrities to create a ceremony that will bind Americans together in a spasm of hate and vengeance, a festival that takes to extremes the violent and vile emotions elicited in Trump's rallies. Like Trump, Sam is consistently vulgar in act and speech. He strings together others' phrases, slogans, clichés, and dog whistles from centuries of American jingoism, racism, and misogyny. And also like Trump, Sam has no respect for facts: History, he tells Nixon,

> is more or less bunk, as Henry Ford liked to say, as saintly and wise a pup as this nation's seen since the Gold Rush — the fatal slantindicular futility of Fact! Appearances, my boy, appearances! Practical politics consists in ignorin' facts! Opinion ultimately rules the world!

Uncle Sam has no use for history, but the Americana Coover puts in Sam's mouth demonstrate that the enmities and violence he elicits are not new in 1953 but old features of American culture. In Coover's conceit, U.S. presidents are "Incarnations" of Uncle Sam. Donald Trump is the most recent but not original.

Coover's vernacular populist Sam is not the old man on military recruiting posters but a sexualized macho

Superhero whose way of baptizing future Presidents is forcibly sodomizing them, as he does Nixon. When Ethel is burned, her body flapping in the air, the description is full of misogynistic sadism as the crowd's erotic burnings stoked by Sam are satisfied. The Rosenbergs are mostly presented in prison, which becomes a metaphor for a country where power takes the form of a bully thug buggering America, an obscene image you may not be ready — yet — to associate with Trump even if he has proudly stated that he grabs pussy whenever he wants and that he is hugely equipped. Like hypocritical Sam, Trump claimed to be the saving embodiment of old patriarchal power — personal, national, and religious. The last, association with Christian righteousness, was perhaps Trump's greatest deception, reeling in evangelical voters just as Sam's burned sacrifice excites the religious in Times Square when the Rosenbergs, Jews like Jesus, are electrically crucified and symbolically raped for the nation's sins.

The Public Burning began as a theater skit and over many years became a marvelous example of Bertholt Brecht's "epic theater" that used "alienation effects" to keep the audience from emotionally identifying too closely with the characters on stage and to force the audience to think about the historical, social, and political systems in which the characters functioned. Coover's alienation devices can be dizzying: feel, think, feel, think, so he includes a character who represents, I believe, the effects he wants to have on his readers. The unnamed character lurches out of *House of Wax*, a 3-D movie playing in New York City at the time of the executions. Still wearing his disorienting 3-D glasses and stumbling through Times Square, the character is able to understand some of the ritual going on but also wails "BEWARE THE MAD ARTIST." Coover is an enraged artist who alienates readers with what seem to be crazed excesses in order to reveal the buried psychological and archetypal motives that produce the burning in the novel and in America, both then and now — the resentful nationalistic crowd's burning need for revenge on the "other," politicians' heated desire to manipulate the crowd's thoughtless passion, and the incineration of nuclear war that may be the end of performance-whipped emotions. Another character, possibly the evil Phantom himself, speaks for rationalists, realists and many reviewers: "'Life's always new and changing, so why fuck it up with all this shit about scapegoats, sacrifices, initiations, saturnalias.'" But these are precisely the elements essential to Coover's achievement, identifying the archaic ghosts in America's machine of civil religion that Trump summoned out of sweaty flesh. His rallies were mocked by the computer-modeling Democrats, but Trump knew, from his own narcissism, what Uncle Sam knew: that people jammed together feel free to abandon their better selves for passionate id-iocy [sic].

No matter how "MAD" Coover is about mass manipulation and mass hysteria, he remains the "ARTIST," both performing and deconstructing performing. He realized that "Envoutements have been known to destroy the priests who practiced them," as performing characters are destroyed in several of his short stories, and yet he was willing to risk the excoriating reviews he received to give America what I think is its most profound political novel, one that exhaustively anatomizes the 1950s and casts ahead to 2016 and beyond with its anthropological insight and ethnographic detail. Coover includes a scene in which Arthur Miller, sitting in a theater where *The Crucible* is showing, muses that "Art is not as lethal as it might be." The aggravated assault and battery of *The Public Burning* come very close to "lethal" art as Coover does his damnedest to kill off the American myths of moral exceptionalism and providential favor by demonstrating the profane backside of the sacred so often invoked by demagogue politicians.

I have merely sketched here the deep and wide achievement of *The Public Burning*. If you would like to learn more, I was one of the few reviewers who praised it (in *The New Republic*, if you still have issues from 1977 around), and I wrote about it in detail in *The Art of Excess*. With limited space here, I have also merely skimmed off the most obvious ways Coover's fiction anticipates our world of fact. If you have followed the rise of Trump — the scandals, the frauds, the cruelties, the buffoonery — reading *The Public Burning* you will find scores of amusing and instructive details that demonstrate Coover's prescience and give you an historical lens through which to see Uncle Sam's new boy in office who looked, on the day he visited President Obama, as if Uncle Sam had had his way with the Donald's butt.

I've written this essay for fiction readers, but also for fiction writers, particularly those too young to have encountered *The Public Burning*. I hope that American novelists will be inspired by Coover's rage and courage, his attention to the deepest structures of public life, and the inventive methods he uses to break through the scrim of conventional political novels. Trump has consistently attacked journalists, the people who uncovered many of the facts employed in *The Public Burning*. He has also attacked dramatic artists who, like Coover, mock fakery and ignorance. We need novelists who will defend fact-gatherers and performers, novelists who will attack with heroic fictions the manifold fictions of Trumpism. Since Trump is easily offended and enraged, an epic of mockery like *The Public Burning* might seduce him into some tweeted stupidity that not even he could lie his way out of. But even if a mock-epic novel cannot bring down a president, can't be "lethal," it can rally the demagogue's opponents and become a text of resistance, as *Catch-22* was during the Vietnam War.

Some left-leaning novelists who have written recent books with epic scale include John Sayles (*A Moment in the Sun*), Garth Risk Hallberg *(City on Fire)*, and William Vollmann. Perhaps they will enlist in the war on Trump. Unfortunately, the best current example of Coover's rage and range is by a British writer, who has his own right-wing problems at home: *Jerusalem* by Alan Moore. Its 1200-plus pages rival *The Public Burning* for functional excess as Moore drills deep into the history and myths of his native Northampton. It would take little effort for readers to contrast the informed empathy of Moore for the left-behind of industrial England with the fake sympathy of the billionaire Trump for unemployed Americans. All of these novels were many years in the making. Maybe the quick-writing Vollmann, if he recovers from his carpal tunnel syndrome, will produce something before Trump runs for a second term. Vollmann's books about historical figures and contemporary prostitutes should serve him well if he produces an epic of America tainted by Trump.

In *The Public Burning* there are all manners of burning. What I didn't find was the meaning of "burned," as in misled and cheated. Perhaps that word is so obvious it need not be remarked in a culture ruled by performance, and yet it is still my final word. With the election of Trump, we need *The Public Burned*.

DONALD TRUMP WON'T READ THIS

Not because he can't read, as the comedian Samantha Bee claimed after reviewing a Trump deposition in which he refused to read aloud language in a contract. He first claimed he forgot his glasses. Then he said he paid lawyers to read the complicated verbiage he wouldn't enunciate. But clearly he can read as he has shown when using a teleprompter, though he feels constrained by the technology.

Not because he has read everything worth reading. A few years ago he claimed to have read a score of books on China. He has also praised at every opportunity Remarque's *All Quiet on the Western Front*. He has said that the Bible is his favorite book, though he didn't offer any evidence that he had read much or any of it. His name appears as author of 14 books that he recommends whenever the occasion arises, but he has also confessed that he hasn't read all of them, so there's plenty left that he has "written" for him to read.

Not because he doesn't have time, though that is the excuse he most often offers when asked what books he has read or is reading. He prefers digests to reports, summaries of digests are even better, and oral briefing is best. He has offered several reasons why he doesn't need to read lengthy texts full of facts and statistics. He has said he is "smart," gets the "gist" quickly, and possesses a lot of "common sense." Like Bush, Trump trusts his gut, his intuition, the accumulated wisdom of his years and experience.

Not because this essay will become in future paragraphs critical of the way Trump processes information. He is very much aware, even obsessively aware, of criticism as long as it comes through sources other than print, particularly television. He has said he gets his information from "the shows," and it has been reported that televisions tuned to Fox News and CNN are constantly on in his office. He apparently watches *Saturday Night Live* whenever Alec Baldwin is mocking him and then deems the show unwatchable. But those desperate open letters to the president-elect from the pundits in *The New York Times*? No chance he'll read them.

Trump won't read this because he associates reading with elites and experts, with the documents and briefing books written by the Intelligence services and the Military, both of which he has mocked as less informed than he. Also, his political enemies, such as the Clintons but particularly Obama, are known as readers, not just of Twitter but of actual books, bound or digital. Even George Bush, no intellectual heavyweight, read books in a competition with Karl Rove. If Trump did read a new book, he probably wouldn't admit it for fear of alienating his base.

Trump won't read this because he's an elder, a patriarch, a heroic savior of the nation. Trump resents learning anything he doesn't already know or can't easily absorb in the fashion he chooses. Like many a grumpy grandfather with not that many years left, Trump craves respect and honor, not just for Trump the brand but for Trump the man, the old man. His ego was outsized because of his accomplishments, no matter how crude or crooked they were. That ego got supersized by age.

As a fellow septuagenarian, I know the attraction of not reading even though — or because — my job is reading. But my job is an old one, reviewing new novels, which, after 50 years of reading them, rarely seem that new, that informative. Trump has a new job as president. It would seem to require that he, a former real estate developer and television personality, accept new ways of acquiring information and reaching judgments, difficult as cognitive change may be after 70. He does not use a computer, the device that can produce out of thin air a fearful library of texts to read. His son Barron can probably reprogram the VCR in the White House, but Trump's resistance to digital information is symbolic of his elder hubris.

But age can diminish one's cognitive and expressive capabilities. David Brooks, in a column entitled "The Snapchat Presidency of Donald Trump," has described the transience and vacuity of his spoken discourse, the unconsidered blurts, unhinged sentences, and fumbled diction. The journalist Jack Shafer submitted some Trump prose to the Flesch-Kincaid grade-level test that showed Trump expressed himself on a third-grade level. And some of those primary-school words were more suitable for the playground than for the classroom. Psychologists and cognitive scientists who have analyzed his speech — the word salad, the internal contradictions, the forgetfulness (or lying) — wondered if Trump might suffer from ADHD or from the beginning of dementia.

Reading this far, you may feel like Trump would probably respond if he made it all the way down here to paragraph eight: "I know all this. Sad!" Here is a new idea: Trump is pre-literate. Not literally, for he graduated from college. He is capable of writing those tweets he sends late at night and early in the morning when, presumably, his staff is not in bed with him. I mean "pre-literate" as Walter Ong uses the term in a profound and valuable book entitled *Orality and Literacy*. For those, like Trump, with little time, it is not a long book, about 200 pages. For those suspicious of complicated, elite language, *Orality and Literacy*, first published in 1982, is generally free of academic jargon. But *Orality and Literacy* is what might be called a bookish book, for Father Ong, a Jesuit priest, was a very widely read Ph.D.-holding professor who used his literacy to set out the kind of information — rich in research, original insights, subtle distinctions, linear arguments — that is unlikely to be created in orality or captured in a digest. What follows contradicts that last phrase. However, my digest is not meant to be final words but mediate words that will lead you to read the book itself — if you think my application of Ong's learning to Trump's ignorance offers a useful perspective on the president's consciousness and potential governance.

Before the invention of writing, Ong explains, language was an event. A speech act disappeared as it happened. Words were simple, concrete, specific, close to what Ong calls the "lifeworld." As action, speech was often "agonistic," communication of information but also a display of power such as ordering, bragging, and insulting. Abstractions didn't exist. An early stage of "thinking" arose from sustained speech with another or others, and memory of that speech — the ability to recall it on another occasion — required mnemonic devices, epithets, and formulaic sayings such as we find in oral epics like those credited to Homer before the invention of writing. The form of this pre-literate "thinking" was primarily chronological narrative, stories and genealogies. Narrative was additive rather than subordinative, aggregative rather than analytic, redundant for memorization, competitive. Learning was by apprenticeship, by repetitive imitation rather than study, for there were no texts or manuals to read and refer to if memory failed. "History" was a small set of oral stories. Relations between individuals or groups were continually negotiated and renegotiated in face-to-face contestation because no written laws existed. In this stage of what Ong calls "primary orality," speech was physical power, oration was not merely persuasion but imposition.

The invention of writing made possible what we now call thinking. An expansion of the lexicon brought abstractions and conceptual categories, analysis and synthesis, rigor and precision. Released from the pressure of real-time expression, writers could consider, reconsider, discriminate among alternative possibilities, subordinate one idea to another, eliminate inconsistencies, correct, and revise. Writers could set down words about words, refining the lexicon, creating distinctions, and building structures of thought. Writing could be speculative, not just assertive or combative. After creating their alphabet, the Greeks who followed Homer invented rules for thinking — logic — and then philosophy, scientific disciplines, political systems and the art of rhetoric that could be applied to both oral and written communications.

"The limits of my language mean the limits of my world," Wittgenstein said. Trump's use of language frequently corresponds to the speech acts of the pre-literate, not only because Trump's discourse is so often rudimentary in diction and "agonistic" in tone but because it rolls out in an additive, often repetitive swirl not disciplined by the protocols of thinking established by writing. At his rallies, he would abandon a written, linear speech on his teleprompter to ad lib a looping and sometimes loopy stream of anecdotes, name-calling, bragging, formulas, inconsistencies, threats, repetitions, hyperbole, random associations and other characteristics of pre-literate speech. He was the master of bombast and bullying that he encouraged his thousands of apprentices to imitate in their speech acts. For Trump, "history" was the stories he could tell, whether true or not. He would deliver remarks as if speaking in a pre-literate time when there were no devices to record his voice — and would then deny what had been recorded as if his words disappeared.

While writing this, I watched Trump's first press conference as president-elect. He spoke to the gathered press the same way he spoke at his rallies — with all the pre-literate clutter and repetition and pugnacity of a mind not formed by reading. One journalist compared Trump's performance to the preliminary shows put on by professional wrestlers, those show-biz fakes who are supposed to remind us of pre-literate warriors. Few people can "think" as well on their feet as they can at their keyboard, and politicians want to have an emotional effect, but Trump's performance before crowds is not different in kind from any of his non-scripted public communication.

Journalists in *The New Republic* and *Bloomberg* have noted how social media, particularly Twitter, resemble Ong's stage of "primary orality" and are therefore ripe for exploitation by Trump's linguistic practices. But his pre-literate language in conversations and even in formal interviews — not just on Twitter — raises several questions that I think are more important than how new media contributed to his election: does Donald Trump "think" in the way that readers think? If not, why might Trump, despite living in a literate age, have a pre-literate mind? And what are the dangers posed by a pre-literate president?

Not faced with another person and not subject to emotional cues, the reader's mind can process a textual message, particularly an emotionally sensitive message, with more detachment than is possible in an oral situation. Readers can choose the speed of processing, decide if they want to read again a particular passage, break the message into its constituent parts, can judge the quality of diction, examine the consistency of the whole message, weigh the message against other information, establish with research in other written documents the truth of the message, and judge the relevance of the message to a situation that may not personally involve the readers. Experienced readers also develop an ability to distinguish hierarchies of reliability, understand the differences between mainstream journalism and tabloid gossip, between, say, *The Nation* and *The National Enquirer*, sourced news and fake news.

In a remarkable interview with *The New York Times* book critic Michiko Kakutani during the last days of his presidency, Obama mentioned many of the books he had read at different stages of his life, credited them with the formation of his character, and discussed how reading helped him as president. Biographies of public figures such as Lincoln and Mandela gave historical context to insistent contemporaneity. Literary fiction taught empathy with people unlike the president. But it was not just "content" that reading provided. The president said that reading allowed him to "slow down and get perspective" and "to get out of his own head."

The literate mind represented by Obama cultivates impersonality. The pre-literate mind is first and foremost personal, always fast to defend or offend. Because this mind is inescapably personal, emotions limit a pre-literate person's ability to process information in ways that will lead to a reasonable, because disinterested, conclusion or judgment. It is this mode of impersonal literate thinking that appears to elude Trump, and why he is so often compared to an infant or child, one, I would suggest, who has not yet learned to read. *The New Yorker* cover of Jan. 23 that pictures a big-headed Trump jammed into a child's ride and honking the car's horn perfectly captures the elderly child-man. Trump seems to immediately process incoming information as offensive to or supportive of his person. He shoots from the hip first, asks questions later, and usually refuses to admit or correct errors.

Trump's response to the possibility that the Russian government had hacked Democrats and used that hacked information to promote Trump's election is indicative of his pre-literate processing. He could not entertain the hack as a speculative possibility, as a reader might. He could not wait for textual data that might prove or disprove the accusation. He could not distance his own defensive ego from the issue, as a reader might. He would not read the evidence. No, he responded as the pre-literate person would with a series of denials and insults that sounded very much like a third-grader, one who may not be reading at grade level. Trump's supporters praise him for "telling it like it is," but third-grade diction is not sufficient to tell any "it" beyond the nine-year-old's world.

I am not questioning Trump's intelligence, which he rates as sky-high. I'm not saying he should be literary. I am saying that his intelligence, his neural circuitry or hardware, has been influenced only weakly by the software of reading-based thinking. How a man born and educated in the middle of the twentieth century could be pre-literate is a question for future biographers with access to his papers and to informants not afraid of speaking about him. From what I have read, Trump seems to have been very competitive, even combative as a child. He was placed in a military school and prided himself on being a tough guy as he believed his father was. A psychologist writing about Trump in *The Atlantic* describes him in some detail as a "warrior." To the psychological background, biographers add his social context: the rough and tumble world of New York property development where, as Trump has written, the art of the deal required the intimidating and relentless oral negotiation that those who have dealt with Trump report. He left the writing and reading of documents and contracts to his accountants and lawyers. He brought his person and pre-literate bluster to the table. That the pre-literate "thinking" he trusted was sometimes wrong and resulted in huge business losses seems not to have changed Trump's way of processing information. It and his trust in voters who didn't read all those newspapers that endorsed

Clinton got him elected despite fears of how a pre-literate person would manage to govern. His answer at his press conference to a question about releasing his taxes summarized the most basic response of the pre-literate man to any question: "I won."

What should worry citizens is the combination of Trump's resistance to the complex information supplied by textuality and his "temperament," his need to treat differences, no matter how petty, as "agonistic," as an occasion to lash out with no apparent second thought. Second and third thoughts are, by the way, made more likely by the distancing effect learned from reading. His anxious supporters say that this double whammy of ignorance and temperament will be moderated or modulated by those around him. What is then worrisome is how Trump's pre-literate mind might be manipulated for political or personal gain by more conventionally informed advisers such as Stephen Bannon and Jared Kushner. Not for no reason does the phrase "have one's ear" imply suspicious influence. The reading eye is the defense against the intimate whisperers.

As I've said, the reader and writer can have second thoughts, can question what they have read or said. Is it necessary to understand Trump as pre-literate? Perhaps not. Readers may be satisfied with psychological or sociological analysis. But I maintain that the anthropological tools of Walter Ong give us a deep and historical perspective on Trump's idiosyncrasies and tropisms, his compulsive behaviors. In a previous essay, I have recommended the best contemporary literary work that "explains" the Trump phenomenon — Robert Coover's anthropology-influenced novel *The Public Burning*. Now I can recommend the best literary work I know about the perils of pre-literate consciousness. Not recommend to Trump, who couldn't or wouldn't read ten pages of it, but to those who want to see dramatized in concrete, even bloody terms the kind of mind Trump brings to the presidency. Like Trump, you don't even have to read all of this book. Just a few chapters of *The Iliad* should do the trick.

The capriciousness and immediacy of pre-literate "thinking" rule the world of *The Iliad*, for its gods are, like the humans, oral creatures subject to no laws except force. The gods' interventions in human affairs are impulsive or whimsical, often inconsistent with previous behavior, and frequently issue from petty, highly personal motives such as perceived insults and combative jealousies. The gods define themselves, as the humans do, in narratives, stories about past glories or frustrations. Fate is the product of competing narratives, not a concept arising out of what we would call causal analysis. Neither gods nor humans can escape their fates, so consciousness concentrates on how to live one's fate as heroically as possible. Personal honor is all, on Olympus or at Troy, in life or death.

The protagonist of *The Iliad*, Achilles, is a man whose wrath at being personally insulted extended the Trojan War. Deprived by Agamemnon of a woman "spoil of war" for whom he lusted and felt entitled, Achilles sulks in his tent, refuses to fight, and insults fellow Greeks who try to make peace between him and Agamemnon. In these scenes, we see orality as *agon*, speech as information but also as a pompous display of itself as power. There is a certain rationality to the demands of Achilles, given the warrior ethos of the Greek city states, but his wrath — more the product of dishonor or shame than loss of the woman — precludes a pragmatic response. He seems governed by a sudden and capricious decision that he cannot bring himself to reverse without dishonoring himself. For him, vengeance is necessary. So only wrath at the death of his friend, Patroclus, brings Achilles into the action that defeats the Trojans and results in his own death, fated but honorable as Achilles takes care to boast.

Only one male character in *The Iliad* explicitly critiques the primary value — personal honor — in the poem's pre-literate culture: the deformed soldier Thersites, who appears just once. A commoner, Thersites can be seen as an early satirist, known for his ability to make his fellow soldiers laugh. He mocks at length the noble Agamemnon for leading the Greeks to a seemingly endless war over a personal insult, the loss of Helen, and for keeping more than his fair share of the spoils. Thersites asks the Greeks to rebel against their leader and return home, but Odysseus, also a noble, intercedes, mocks Thersites, beats him and defends the honor of Agamemnon, himself, and all Greek nobles. For centuries, readers of *The Iliad* agreed with Odysseus, perhaps because Thersites is depicted as physically ugly and because he is not a "warrior" capable of backing up the force of his words with physical force. But there have been readers who see in Thersites — described by Odysseus as λιγὺς αγορητής (literally "clear-toned speaker in the agora") and as "eloquent," "fluent," and "witty" by various translators — Homer's criticism of the pre-literate culture of honor, force, and vengeance that controls the poem. To the contemporary reader, the club-footed Thersites is the deconstructive stand-in for the poet (blind in legend) who has only spoken words to exert influence.

In *The Public Burning*, the Trump figure is Uncle Sam, a con man whose linguistic displays are chosen as stratagems of power. In *The Iliad,* characters do not choose pre-literate utterances. They are, according to Ong, how the people spoke and, therefore, "thought." Their language was, in a way, their fate, inescapable before writing expanded the resources of spoken discourse. Trump is frightening as a president — as the supposed model of reasoned governance — because pre-literate speech and its pre-thinking seem to be with him as intrinsic — as fated — as they were for Greeks thousands of years ago. Obsessed with personal honor, capricious, wrathful and bombastic,

Donald Trump is a throwback, not just to the age of fifties Mad Men or nineteenth-century con men or the foolish men in the Feast of Fools but much further back to the oral men whose pre-literate "thinking" most civilizations — and their leaders — have left behind.

Just before leaving office, reader-in-chief Obama had lunch with Junot Diaz, Dave Eggers, Barbara Kingsolver, Zadie Smith, and Colson Whitehead. Would that Obama were recruiting them to write novels about Trump. Though none is likely to compose a contemporary *Iliad*, their novels do demonstrate that the writers all have the historical and cross-cultural knowledge to place Trump in context. Kingsolver and Eggers could be strong environmental and technological critics. Diaz, Smith, and Whitehead can address the racism surrounding Trumpism. Whitehead also has a strain of the fantastic displayed in *The Intuitionist*, his zombie novel *Zone One*, and in his literalization of metaphor in *The Underground Railroad*. If not an epic, Whitehead might write magic realism about Trump the magus. The women know misogyny. The men are nimble satirists. Perhaps the Obama Five will form a Team Thersites to contest Trump the self-styled "warrior" and demagogue with an Achilles heel of petty pride.

SYSTEMS NOVELISTS WE NEED NOW

In Joshua Cohen's recent novel *Book of Numbers*, a character wants to engineer "the ultimate. The connection of connections." Since the assertion in *Gravity's Rainbow* that "everything is connected," Cohen's "ultimate" has been the aim of the "systems novel," a form I defined and promoted in two books — *In the Loop* and *The Art of Excess* — published in the late 1980s. *In the Loop* was about all of Don DeLillo's work through *White Noise*. *The Art of Excess* treated individual novels of the 1970s and 80s: *Gravity's Rainbow* (the master text), Heller's *Something Happened*, Gaddis's *JR*, Coover's *The Public Burning*, McElroy's *Women and Men*, Barth's *LETTERS*, and Le Guin's *Always Coming Home*. These books were long and seemed to some readers excessive, but I argued their bulk enabled their authors to present the anthropological, historical, environmental, economic, political, technological, or social systems in which the novels' characters had their lives and plots. Systems novels, as much of DeLillo's work demonstrates, don't have to be lengthy. But they do need to extend intellectually beyond what DeLillo called "around the house-and-in-the-yard" fiction, novels with limited purviews rooted in journalistic observation and psychological interpretation. Why we need such works now I will get to shortly.

Many of the novels I treated were influenced by Ludwig von Bertalanffy's "systems theory," usually indirectly as the biologist's ideas percolated through other disciplines. Chief among those ideas was Bertalanffy's emphasis on the role of information and feedback (connections of connections) in the creation of biological and other systems. This is a truism now but was new when Bertalanffy was attempting to define the abstract principles of systems formation across different sciences. Bertalanffy claimed his "systems theory" created a new paradigm. I claimed that its influence on fiction writers created a new kind of fiction, the "systems novel," that, I further claimed, was particularly adept at and possibly necessary for representing a contemporary world of complex, interlocking systems such as those present in, for example, *Gravity's Rainbow* or, more modestly, in *White Noise*, both of which use the language of cybernetic systems.

The systems novels of the twentieth century were formally, as well as intellectually, ambitious, experimenting with structures and styles that would call attention to and represent the avant-garde conceptual systems central to the books. It's this systemic ambition that I've been using as a touchstone when reviewing hundreds of novels since I published those two critical studies more than 25 years ago. And that touchstone is probably why I'm frequently disappointed in the works that I'm assigned or find on the National Book Awards list of finalists, and why I seem at times, even to myself, a superannuated crank. But then some young writer, influenced by Pynchon or DeLillo or Gaddis, comes along to renew the systems novel and my confidence in it. David Foster Wallace was such a writer. Richard Powers is another. Also William Vollmann. Their *Infinite Jest* and *Gold Bug Variations* and *You Bright And Risen Angels*, all of which allude to *Gravity's Rainbow* and seem influenced by DeLillo, are the equals of that earlier generation's grand (and excessive) accomplishments.

Powers's most recent novel is *Orfeo*, a brief coda to his earlier systems fiction, and a possible harbinger of larger work to come. Two younger novelists — Tom McCarthy and Joshua Cohen — have emerged with systems novels informed by cutting edge information about information processing. I reviewed all of these books when they came out. Those reviews are slightly retouched here as I bring them together to evaluate the current health of the systems novel and to speculate about who might write such a novel about Trump — one that would give us a profound understanding of what produced him and of what readers, with that understanding, could do to resist him.

***

Since reviewing Powers's second novel, *Prisoner's Dilemma,* in 1988, I've had to keep track of his age so that, when asked who to read, I can say, "Powers. He's the most important living American novelist under" whatever age he happens to be at the time. At this writing, he's 56, and I believe only (in alphabetical order) DeLillo, Morrison, Pynchon, and Roth — all two decades older — stand above him. Of novelists in Powers's generation with whom he is often compared — Franzen, Vollmann, Wallace — none equals Powers's combination of consistent production, intellectual range, formal ingenuity, and emotional effect.

Powers has now published eleven novels and won the National Book Award for *The Echo Maker* in 2007, and yet he remains unknown and intimidating territory to many readers. *Orfeo* seems designed to reach a wider audience and is an excellent introduction to his concerns in earlier books. Powers novels usually achieve their depth through parallax, splicing together two eras or several stories or different systems of information: World War I in Holland and contemporary Boston in *Three Farmers on Their Way to a Dance;* programmers developing a virtual reality cave in Seattle and a hostage struggling to survive in Beirut in

Plowing the Dark; two love stories, Bach, and genetics in two separate decades in *The Gold Bug Variations*.

Orfeo is different. It tells the life of one contemporary character, Peter Els, a seventy-year-old composer and retired music professor; initially fits the now-established genre of the bioterrorism thriller; and follows a linear plot that transpires over a couple of weeks. A chemistry student in college, Peter has bought equipment that allows him to engineer pathogenic bacteria in his Pennsylvania home. When Homeland Security hears of this and raids, Peter flees, first hiding out alone and then seeking out persons from his past. His former therapist and lover gives him a smartphone with a GPS to help his flight. His former wife in St. Louis gives him money. His old collaborator in Phoenix lets Peter have his car; and his daughter, who has given him her attention over the last decade despite being abandoned as a child, offers to shelter him in San Francisco. This escape-and-return plot occurs at the end of *Prisoner's Dilemma*, but *Orfeo* has more narrative momentum and suspense — What is Peter's plan for the bacteria? Will he be caught? — than other Powers novels. I can almost see a slimmed-down Frank Langella as Peter Els in the westering road-trip movie.

Orfeo is different but not so different. During the interstate stretches between stops, Powers constructs a biography that shares features with other protagonists' lives in "Powers World," a phrase the author uses in two novels. Like the character named "Powers" in *Galatea 2.2*, Peter attends college to study science and then disappoints his father by switching to art — to music. Also like "Powers," he falls in love at the University of Illinois, moves with his lover to Boston (where one becomes a museum guard), dedicates himself to his art, and loses his lover. Then, like the biologist Ressler in *The Gold Bug Variations*, who gives up science at Illinois for music composition, Peter goes to New York and takes marginal jobs. He has a little success with his experimental compositions, but Peter eventually withdraws for a decade to a Unabomber-like existence in a New Hampshire cabin before taking a teaching job at a small college in Pennsylvania. Although Peter has contacts with various movements in music — John Cage's "musicircus" at Illinois, mixed-media extravaganzas, downtown New York minimalism in the 1980s, computer-generated performances — his story is personal, specific. *Orfeo* and Peter have plenty of ideas about music, but Peter is primarily a complex individual, grappling for decades with families lost and friendships tested, secondarily a representative artist whose vocation can't support him in an age of mass media. His life is sometimes heroic, sometimes foolish, occasionally comic, and eventually sad. That's when Peter starts composing new bacteria.

As *Orfeo* illustrates, Powers's work is most fundamentally about systemic recombination. Genetics is the source and model, mentioned in his first book, most explicit in *The Gold Bug Variations*, crucial in his last novel, *Generosity*, and a force in *Orfeo*, but the repetition and variation of genetics are also present in other constituents of Powers World: musical history in *Orfeo*, computer programming in several books, even the flight of cranes in *The Echo Maker*. And the eleven novels, as I've suggested with just a few examples, are themselves recombinant systems, twisting like the double helix character types and common themes from one novel to another, turning and returning to situations, examining similar lives from different perspectives.

The importance of Powers that I so baldly asserted earlier issues from the variety, interpretive power, and contemporaneity of the systems he employs, which are usually scientific. Game theory, chaos theory, cognitive connectionism, oncology, relativity physics, and evolutionary psychology are some of the disciplines and systems Powers uses to understand — and expand — what it means to be human. In *The Echo Maker*, for example, he establishes deep analogies between neurology and ecology. Put simply, Powers knows more about systems than other novelists of his generation and knows how to use his prodigious expertise to place substantial, thoughtful characters in "the intricate, ingenious forms" (to quote Peter) that Powers's best fictions create to imitate the information they contain. In *Generosity* a character runs through a list of words deriving from the old Latin gens: gene, genius, ingenuity, and generosity are the ones most applicable to Powers and his World.

In *Orfeo* it's bacteria that Powers knows as both a basis of human life and, in certain drug-resistant mutations, a danger to human lives. For this book, Powers seems to have been reading Jared Diamond's *Guns, Germs, and Steel*. Powers gives Peter and readers just enough information to establish the threat of bioterrorism and to spring the plot, but bacteria function more as a metaphor than a full-fledged intellectual perspective of the kind I've mentioned. Listening to his car radio, Peter finds the coarsening of discourse and music an all-over, all-the-time phenomenon like bacteria. Equally pervasive, invisible, and invasive is the government's ability to trace a citizen's interests and movements through surveillance of his entries into the electronic web. But the primary target of Powers's bacteriological metaphor is the omnipresent "growth industry" in fear that an American media environment of constant threat nourishes like food left too long out of the refrigerator. Powers uses the phrase "Age of Bacteria," but Age of Panic might have been truer to the contemporary reportage he incorporates into *Orfeo*. In mythic terms, the cultural critique in the novel pits Orpheus, the master of calming music, versus Pan, the god of mass fear.

For all of Powers's knowledge of and respect for up-to-the-minute scientific systems, he often suspects their tendency to philosophical reductionism and to harmful technological application. One of Peter's first compositions used the closing sections of Whitman's "Song of Myself." Late in the novel, Powers has Peter return to those lines and identify with Whitman, an artist who welcomed the influence of sciences but finally celebrated the open road and open — but still inviolate — self. Whitman also nicely contributes to the panic and bacterial themes of *Orfeo*, for one of the fearless poet's last lines, which Powers quotes twice, is: "If you want me again, look for me under your boot soles."

From Powers, a novel entitled *Orfeo* is no surprise. In *Galatea 2.2*, a character points out that "Orphic Rewards" is an anagram of the author's name, and Powers mentions numerous operas about Orpheus in *The Time of Our Singing*, his novel about African-American musicians. Think of Orpheus as an example of repetition and variation: he wanted to save Eurydice from the underworld and repeat their earthly love but failed because he looked back. Like Orpheus, many protagonists in Powers World are frustrated saviors in contemporary hells. The doctor and nurse in the inner-city hospital of *Operation Wandering Soul* try to save the lives of very sick children; the protagonists of *Generosity* attempt to prevent an unnaturally happy woman from exploitation by Faustian genetic engineers.

Peter is also a would-be savior, a foiler of death. He describes a youthful composition in both Orphic and Powers terms: "He borrowed from voices dead for centuries and made them chatter posthumously. And he repeated, recombined, and looped everything until the whole was wide enough to stretch from dawn to dusk." Discouraged by the tepid reception of his early music, Peter writes a song his daughter and wife love and thinks, "A dozen such tunes over the course of a career, and he might even have saved lives." In the novel's present, Peter wants to somehow encode beautiful music in bacteria to save it and, more unlikely, save listeners from the barbaric noise constantly in their ears.

In keeping with the principle of recombination, Peter's bacterium of choice — "Serratia marcescens. It looked like blood seeping out of old food" — was discovered by Pythagoras long ago. The red bacterium is also something of a red herring in the plot, which I won't spoil like the food. The "Orphic Reward" of the novel is less in soteriological music than in Peter's cross-country journey: the mythic musician as senior citizen looking back on and attempting to make amends with loved ones — mostly women — from his past whom, like Eurydice, Peter betrayed or allowed to drift away from him. The protagonists in Powers World are usually younger than their creator. In *Orfeo* Powers adds a character fourteen years his senior to the ever-increasing rogues gallery of guilty old men — such as William Gass's music professor in *Middle C* — that American novelists have been assembling in recent years. Powers has been criticized for imagining protagonists who do not "live" or who elicit little affect. If life is motion, as Faulkner said, Peter moves around and should move readers with his desires and regrets — but even more with his late-life spark and reconnections.

Powers has a novelist in *Generosity* say, "A story with no end or impediment is no story at all." *Orfeo* has one impediment and two endings. For readers without considerable knowledge of symphonic, chamber, and operatic music, Powers's descriptions of performances, both actual and invented by him for Peter, will be difficult, necessary to communicate Peter's passion but still an impediment the author attempts to finesse by describing listeners' emotional responses along with the structure of the music. Here an example, Peter listening to Steve Reich's *Proverb* in a student café:

> *The echoing lines slow to half speed, reprising the song's first measures. Augmentation, it was called once, worlds ago, before MIDI. The two-part canon turns into a trio. Choir-boy clarity thickens, then smears out as thin as gold leaf…. The couple at the next table freeze, alerted. The woman's soul is all up in her ears. The boy leans forward in a frightened crouch; someone is doing a thing better than he ever will.*

More rewarding for the non-musical are Powers's reflections on music and animals, and numerous anecdotes about composers such as Shostakovich and Messiaen, who wrote music while facing a possible death sentence, or Harry Partch, a Whitmanian figure who composed in extreme poverty.

About the two endings: one is literal, the other figurative. From the beginning, very short texts in a different font seem dropped at random into the novel. They are sometimes statements readers can identify as Peter's, sometimes quotations that can be Googled, but only near the end of the novel do readers find out the source and occasion of these texts. Although they are not a fully developed alternative to the novel's plot and backstory, the micro-passages do introduce some of the dissonance and parallax of earlier books. And they are another example of bacterial replication as they geometrically increase when picked up by and spread through the system of social media. Powers used a similar strategy of narrational concealment in *The Gold Bug Variations*, where readers discover on the last page the actual producers of much of the text. The effect of this concealment in *Orfeo*, for me at least, is rereading the novel from a new perspective and coming to the end a second time, another example of Powers's guiding principle of repetition and variation.

Powers uses the term "coda" in *Orfeo*, and it seems to be a coda to the remarkable novels that precede it, as the last lines of "Song of Myself" are a coda, a leave-taking. In music, a coda ends a movement or piece and looks back on the composition. Another genetics-influenced systems novelist, John Barth, created a maximalist coda in his *LETTERS*, his seventh novel, which includes characters from his previous six. Powers's coda is simpler and shorter, with the thick verisimilitude of *The Echo Maker* and *Generosity* thinned out to essentials of plot and character. Though Powers is not yet sixty, the language he uses has the tension of what Edward Said called "the late style," a discord between still-passionate resistance to wisdom and a lean diction of resignation.

The ending of *Orfeo* may be the Orphic end of life for Peter, but we will have to wait for Powers's twelfth novel to find out if *Orfeo* is a farewell to his nearly constant subjects — how systems of science and art can coalesce. As an indirect "Song of Myself," *Orfeo* does summarize the author's conflicting motivations in his novelistic career, wanting early, like Peter in his twenties and thirties, to produce unique and therefore necessarily dissonant or difficult work but also wanting, like Peter as a youth and as an older man, to produce work that many might love. *Orfeo* and the three novels that precede it tip toward increasing accessibility, and at least the National Book Award judges loved *The Echo Maker*, and yet in *Orfeo* one also senses that the author has once more descended into Powers Underworld with the hope of finding a muse who would inspire him to create what may be impossible art, fiction both systemic and particular, profound and popular. What I hope to see from him is another *Gain* about how Big Business violates little lives.

***

Tom McCarthy's fourth novel is a cautionary tale about cultural generalizations, but I'll advance one anyway: If the most popular British male novelists, such as Ian McEwan and Martin Amis, are essentially artful sociologists, younger and more deep-diving authors — David Mitchell, Hari Kunzru, Tom McCarthy — are novelistic anthropologists. The trio have different interests: Mitchell in cross-cultural and historical homologies, Kunzru in modes of cultural disappearance and "transmission" (to use the title of his second novel), and McCarthy in the relations among the systems of technology, high culture, and pop culture (he has published a post-structuralist analysis of *Tintin*). In *Satin Island*, McCarthy's anthropologically influenced systems approach to contemporary life is more explicit than ever, for his protagonist/narrator is a doctorate-holding, generalization-generating ethnographer.

The fortyish character, who calls himself "U.," reveals next to nothing about his life before he became an anthropologist. He lives alone, has no contact with family, and works for an unnamed British consulting firm — "the Company" — on the Koob-Sassen Project, a massive venture of "network architecture" that "was very abstract," even "invisible" to the populace. U. has never been to New Guinea or Amazonia. He sits in a basement office and conducts his "research" mostly by cruising media and intuiting memes before they trend. He reports his findings to the Company's chief executive, Peyman, a cross between charismatic Steve Jobs and wonky Malcolm Gladwell, a powerful font of counterintuitive but highly marketable ideas. U. would be satisfied to follow his whimsical interests, collecting and communicating "data," for example, on parachute accidents and oil spills, but Peyman has tasked him with writing the "Great Report," a summation of the age. Since the contemporary period is as amorphous and murky as oil and sea water, U. becomes increasingly desperate to create an original form that would conceptualize the epoch. Changes in U.'s thinking, emotions, and language as he attempts to compose the Report supply McCarthy with a narrative, if not exactly a plot. Of "events," U. says in chapter 2, "If you want those, you'd best stop reading now."

Because U. has no name, tries to "map" an enigmatic phenomenon, and sees the gantries of a ferry as "the drawbridge to some castle" he will never enter, he recalls Kafka's K, the land surveyor denied admittance in *The Castle*. But *Satin Island* has fewer characters, less conflict, and, I think, little religious resonance, even though "Peyman" means "god" in urban slang and U. thinks of him as a "god" who withdraws from his creation. U. mentions a colleague who shows him videos, periodically talks with a systems analyst friend dying of thyroid cancer, and has occasional sex with a woman named Madison, but they elicit scant emotional response from U.

Emerson said the scholar is "Man Thinking," and that's what U., Ph.D. is. "Protagonist Thinking" is a chancy gambit for a novel. McCarthy more than gets away with it for a combination of reasons. U. knows classical anthropologists and recent French theorists and works them into his narration to establish his authority. He's a perceptive observer of cultural minutiae even when readers are rarely sure if his interpretations are insightful or wacky. Though economical with details of office politics, the novel efficiently satirizes the widening influence of consultants, the money-making mad men of blue-sky concepts. Most significantly, U.'s need to create a necessarily abstract "master-pattern" of contemporary culture cleverly represents the modern attraction to grand, totalizing intellectual systems, what Francois Lyotard called in his *The Postmodern Condition* "master narratives." Like Lyotard in that influential book, McCarthy critiques this urge to abstract mastery and its commercial co-opting.

I value Occam's Razor as much as the next guy. Entities should not be multiplied unnecessarily. *Satin Island* can be comfortably called a "novel of ideas" or "systems novel," but it seems to ask for a revised terminology. Since the beginning of his career, McCarthy has been closely affiliated with the world of visual arts, so I assume that he has chosen or approved his novel's cover and that it points to the hybrid nature of his book. The cover's grid is splashed with various colors, some of which shade into each other. Non-fiction terms — treatise, essay, report, confession, and manifesto — straddle boxes in the grid; all except novel are partly cancelled. Outside the grid are the author and title. The splotches imply Abstract Expressionism; most of the terms refer to writing about the real world. Like its cover, then, *Satin Island* is a work of Abstract Realism, a term only slightly different from "systems novel."

U. began his career as a phenomenologist, more a participant in real life than a detached analyst. His first book was about clubbing, for which he did several years of research tending bar, drinking, taking drugs, organizing raves, and hanging out with young people in London. But in the cubicle world of the Company, U. has little contact with people. McCarthy implies the danger of and an alternative to U.'s mediated and abstracted life with the longest continuous section of the novel, a narrative Madison relates about participating in the 2001 Genoa demonstrations against the G8 and globalism. This narrative has "events" and plot. Falsely arrested and assaulted like many others, Madison is taken by the police to a remote estate where she is tortured by a nameless mysterious man who uses a cattle prod to make her perform "postures" he dictates as he receives directions from an electronic device only he can perceive.

McCarthy's concrete descriptions of demonstrations and their aftermath are a late, unexpected burst of history-based realism into the ruminations of *Satin Island*. Madison's story about her torture, though, may have been invented by her to indirectly show U. the danger of his growing separation from flesh-and-blood reality, for the torturer is, like U., a cipher who seems governed by an non-human medium and who makes only ritualistic contact with Madison. It was in Genoa, Madison also tells U., where Nietzsche went mad after seeing a man beating a horse. That U. doesn't heed Madison's stories about emotional response and its lack is no surprise given his directive from Peyman to think globally.

U. wonders if he might pass off *Satin Island* as the "Great Report," but McCarthy's text is actually U.'s unreliable "confession," to use a term from the cover. He retains the form of scientific writing by continuing to number each paragraph in each chapter, but his imagination fills the pages. He daydreams about the "ecstatic reception" his ideas will receive. Not long after, he fantasizes about leading an attack on the "nefarious" Company that has financed the Report. He shows signs of paranoia, fearing the Report has already been written by a software program. His suspect epiphanies begin to seem "miraculous" to him. The climax of U.'s kinked thinking occurs on a trip to New York, where U. is drawn toward Staten Island because it is close in sound to his vivid dream of a Satin Island. Because U. is interested initially in oil spills and since his Satin Island is a vast dump, readers may be led to believe the novel will have an ecological or environmental focus. But as the pages about Staten Island show, *Satin Island* is really more like the anthropologist Gregory Bateson's classic *Steps to an Ecology of Mind*, a work of systems thinking that lists the multiple errors to avoid when trying to construct a linguistic system. *Satin Island* is both systems novel and critique of the thinking underlying systems novels.

In the following passage, U. sits down to begin the Report. He has cleared his desk, made it a "tabula rasa." Now he pictures himself as

> *an industrialist, viewing a clearing in the forest where his factory would go; or as an urban planner, given carte blanche to design from scratch a new, magnificent cosmopolis; a mathematician, a topologist or trigonometrist, contemplating space in its most pure and abstract form; an explorer, sea-discoverer, world-conqueror from centuries gone by, standing at his prow as his dominion-to-be hove into view; this virgin territory that he would shape after himself and make his own.*

This excerpt is more obviously comic than much of the novel, but the passage does reveal the grandiose narcissism that, in an overloaded information system, leads a person to impose a master narrative, any master narrative. Occam's Razor cuts both ways: it reminds one to accept the simplest possible explanation of phenomena but also encourages one to create the highest possible level of abstraction — which may be a fabrication. Because U. in this passage sounds as if he were under pressure to compose the Great American or Great English Novel, *Satin Island* also functions as a metafictional warning. Mapping mastery is the temptation of every novelist who wants his or her work to be more than artful sociology.

Satin Island resembles Don DeLillo's *Point Omega* and several more recent novels about lonely Man Thinking: Teju Cole's *Open City*, Joseph O'Neill's *The Dog*, and Richard Ford's *Let Me Be Frank with You*. McCarthy's novel is the most abstract of these — and the most profound in examining the relation between conceptualizing and fictionalizing. Within McCarthy's oeuvre, *Satin Island* is the flip side of *Remainder*, his first published and best-known novel, in which the protagonist is Man Re-Enacting —

minutely, elaborately, and obsessively replaying concrete scenes from his imagination and life in order to intensely experience their reality. In an influential essay entitled "Two Paths for the Novel," Zadie Smith praised *Remainder* for eschewing the "lyrical realism" represented by Joseph O'Neill's *Netherland*, yet another Man Thinking novel. McCarthy's path was pressing an abstract conceit — reenactment — to risky, shaggy, and then absurd lengths. *Satin Island* is somewhat less willful in its narrator's path toward interpretive mastery, and that path takes him only to foolishness.

McCarthy's other two novels — *Men in Space* and *C* — are more traditional in the illusion they offer that characters, rather than the author, dictate plot, and are, I believe, his best work because of their balance between Abstraction and Realism, system and individuality. The first-written *Men in Space* treats a Bulgarian art forger in Prague and those who would possess the stolen original painting that he has copied twice to confuse his interpreters and pursuers. (Note to Tom McCarthy: yes, I noticed the submerged allusion in *Satin Island* to the Amsterdam shootout in *Men in Space*.) *C* is about an early-twentieth-century Englishman who quests for authenticity beneath layers of cultural copies, as one meaning of its title implies. Like *Remainder* and *Satin Island*, the novels are self-aware fictions — *Men in Space* through its references to visual art, *C* with its interest in early communications systems — but along with their philosophical concerns the books include various characters in conflict, and considerable ethnographic detail of life in several European countries. Because these novels do not seem over-determined by a theory-minded author, *Men in Space* and *C* — like Nietzsche's beaten horse — can elicit the visceral response Zadie Smith objected to in works of "lyrical realism." Since all of McCarthy's novels before *Satin Island* end with violence or death, I think of this fourth fiction as the comedy performed after three tragedies in ancient Greek festivals. Aristophanes never gets the same respect as Sophocles, but *Satin Island* does give McCarthy a niche in the great tradition of intellectual satire stretching from that classical Greek mocker to Swift, Sterne, Kafka, and Beckett. And who knows but that on the higher frequencies, U. may even speak to you or for you. I would love to see McCarthy speak to all of us on the subject of Donald Trump.

***

A latecomer to writing fiction, I'm always on the envious lookout for American novelists whose first books come fulsomely formed in their youth: prodigious works such as William Gaddis's *The Recognitions*, Thomas Pynchon's *V.*, Richard Powers's *Three Farmers on Their Way to a Dance*, William Vollmann's *You Bright and Risen Angels*, Mark Danielewski's *House of Leaves*, three published before their authors were 30, all before 35. Joshua Cohen began in 2007 with *Cadenza for the Schneidermann Violin Concerto*, when he was 27. Now — at 35 — Cohen has published two prodigious novels: *Witz* (2010), an 817-page mock epic about the last Jew in the world, and his new release, *Book of Numbers*, a 580-page novel about the founder of "Tetration," an Internet search company that resembles Google.

The novels of the earlier prodigies above were stuffed with specialized, often technical knowledge, were non-linear in form, and disparate in styles, often more like strange systems of information than traditional narratives. The books asked readers to perform searches: to comb through heterogeneous materials and find connections between historical or scientific information and personal experience. The most recent of the earlier five, *House of Leaves* (2000), is the most directly influenced by information processing: Danielewski's inclusion of visual materials and an index make the book a print simulacrum of a searchable hypertext. *Book of Numbers* is the next generation of the systems novel, for Cohen combines prodigious knowledge and formal disruption to explicitly treat math prodigies who developed the hardware and software to manage massive information — and then surveil the wetware of private lives.

Joshua Cohen, the forty-year-old founder of Tetration and fourteenth-richest man in the world, hires a failed almost-forty novelist, also named Joshua Cohen, to ghostwrite his autobiography. *Book of Numbers* is a combination biography of the founder and autobiography of the ghost, structured as a hard-drive collection of Danielewski-like documents: interview transcripts, formulas, programming code, blog posts by the ghost's estranged wife, emails by her current lover and the ghost's agent, questionable first-person recollections, photos of archaic female forms, fabricated epigraphs, texts that have been crossed through, and one crucial footnote that may deconstruct the whole kludged assemblage.

On the novel's first page, the ghost says that "there's nothing worse than description. . . . No, characterization is worse. No, dialogue is." Not a very welcoming way to start a book. But the ghost soon elicits sympathy: because his novel about the Holocaust was published on 9/11/2001, it flopped. Since then he has been writing book reviews (like author Cohen, a former staff reviewer at *Harper's*) and doing anonymous hack work — travel pieces, restaurant reviews, and corporate speeches — while being supported by his wife. In the novel's present of 2011, she is seeing another man while writing a blog revealing the ghost's many flaws.

Back in 2004, the ghost caught a break from a "Cohencidence" [*Witz*] when asked to interview the celebrity who shares his name, but the piece was killed because it wasn't puffery. Now the founder remembers that interview (which resembles one that the real-life Joshua Cohen did with Slavoj Žižek and offers to pay a huge amount of money to the ghost if he'll write a quick-and-dirty tell-all autobiography. Ghost Cohen says "readable books" must have their research "wrapped like mummies, in the purest and softest verbiage, which both preserves them and makes them presentable." Author Cohen uses about a hundred pages of soft verbiage to establish human interest in his narrator, but I found in these pages to be familiar stuff from — or parody of — too numerous "confessional" novels by frustrated New York City writers.

Harder and much more interesting verbiage begins once the setting moves from New York and Palo Alto to Dubai and Abu Dhabi, where the two Cohens stay in luxury hotels. Here the founder, whom the ghost calls "Principal," narrates his life. His father, Abraham, helped create the personal computer; Principal was a math prodigy who went to Stanford in 1989 but didn't attend classes; Principal and two computer science whizzes created a marginally profitable list of websites and then went on to invent the algorithm for Tetration (which refers, like googolplex, to almost impossibly large numbers and, in this novel about Jewish protagonists, may allude to the Tetragrammaton, the four Hebrew letters transliterated as Yahweh). Tetration needed venture capital, and then an executive — Kori Dienerowitz — to manage the three prodigies, who were joined by a slightly older "computing genius" from India — Muwekma Ohlone, or "Moe" — who added to the search algorithm "reversibility," the ability to store information about the searcher, leading to government surveillance and entrapment of Tetration users. Dying of cancer, Principal has become an ascetic Buddhist with eccentricities like those of Howard Hughes. But Principal wants to publish his autobiography to cleanse his soul, punish those inside the company who betrayed his vision, and expose NSA-type snooping with which Tetration cooperated.

Cohen's amalgam of Bill Gates, Steve Jobs, and the less publicly known founders of Google seems informed and authentic, perhaps because the author gives Principal an authoritative and sometimes authoritarian voice. He uses the royal (or corporate) "we" when talking about himself, has little use for transitions or his ghost's questions, carries a prodigious memory, and spools out speech thick with scientific terminology and what the ghost calls "techsperanto," neologisms such as "rectard," "quadlingual," and "comptrasted." Principal has conflicts with his colleagues, but the arguments are about ideas and rarely personal, for, unlike his ghost, whose life is full of personal problems, Principal back then had little time for or interest in the quotidian. Occasionally impenetrable, Principal's discourse is a remarkable tour de force for a literary novelist.

Part 3 (entitled "1" again following Parts 1 and 2, to highlight the "ones and zeroes" of code) returns to the softer verbiage of the ghost, now separated from Principal, impoverished in Germany, forbidden online access to protect secrecy, and trying to work on the contracted book. There are distractions and complications. He searches in Vienna for a young Omani woman whom he rescued from spousal abuse in Dubai. He reports a threat from a Julian Assange figure — Thor Ang Balk of "b-Leaks" — or maybe from his rogue assistant Anders Maleksen, who wants to leak the information the ghost has before he can publish it in a book. The ghost's agent dies of a heart attack, endangering payment for the book, and the ghost's estranged wife comes back into the picture via her blog, with a story about a betrayal he had not admitted earlier. The ghost, along with the reader, wonders what happened to Principal. These multiple plot points seem to be the author's reward for those literary readers who may have struggled through Principal's math-heavy history of Tetration. Or these plot developments could have been invented by the ghostwriter, to make his combination biography/autobiography salable to a publisher if Principal's book is anticipated by leaks. In a work about contemporaries' unwillingness or inability to keep secrets, narrator Cohen may have "secretly" composed a fiction within author Cohen's novel.

The final words of *Witz* are that being a Cohen "is steady work." *Book of Numbers* employs three different Joshua Cohens and links them by betrayal. The ghost's purely motivated Holocaust novel is betrayed by circumstances. The ghost and his wife lose faith in another. The founder allows his pure mathematics to be betrayed for profit and for governmental cooperation: he is betrayed by his colleagues and, perhaps, his biographer. Author Cohen creates initial expectations of accessibility that are betrayed in part 2 and then restored in part 3.

And then there's that much older (read: biblical) Joshua. In the Old Testament's Book of Numbers, Yahweh feels betrayed by the Israelites who He has delivered from Egypt. He continually punishes them in the wilderness, while denying entry into the Promised Land to Moses, the founder of the code. The spies who came back from the Promised Land with a positive report, Joshua and Caleb (the name given to a journalist turned fiction writer in the novel), are honored by Yahweh, and Joshua leads the Israelites into Canaan. Author Joshua Cohen reverses the biblical Joshua. Here, Cohen is the spy in Silicon Valley who shows it's not all milk and honey. Perhaps in a decade or so, yet another Joshua may emerge from a library to claims there's an encrypted relation between *Book of Numbers* and the *Kabbalah*, where gematria turns letters into numbers, and Cohen's novel will be "betrayed" by its interpreter. Or perhaps not.

Prodigies can be abrasive. Ghost Cohen's and author Cohen's first words are, "If you're reading this on a screen, fuck off." (Danielewski's opening sentence in *House of Leaves* is, "This is not for you.") This novel is for you if you love, as I do, moral complexities that an author scales up and out from personal life into world-influencing systems, from individual identity and marital issues to technology, politics, history, and religion — before looping back down again to show the effects of encompassing systems on the personal. The following passage from one of Principal's transcribed interviews illustrates his limited moral concerns, as well as his quirky style. Cohen the interviewer has asked Principal about Tetration's "censorship of nonillegal sites." Principal replies:

> *If we experienced guilt it was not from violating any ethics or morals but the magnitude of the second eigenvalue. Tetrate it. Do not. Deploying emotions without matrices distressed us. Human intervention was the crime. Lack of system was the crime. This is all about our eternal failure to have deved a viable semantic algy that translates, interprets, and reads between the lines to appreciate intent.*

"Eigenvalue" has to do with the number of variables. "Deved" and "algy" are short for "developed" and "algorithm." "Tetrate" means "search." Only later does Principal admit that it's not the intent of a site's creator that matters but the intent of Big Government's search of the sites that the Big Data of Tetration can identify. Principal failed to develop the algy that "reads between the lines," but author Cohen employs an archaic information system — the novel — that trains readers to do just that and to make subtle moral judgments about loyalty and betrayal, purity and profit. Judgments that require thinking beyond the childish law of Google: "Don't be evil."

In Cohen's previous book, *Four New Messages* (several of which are about the Internet), he has a New York novelist say that in an earlier time people "wrote excessive books about excess that were never excessively read." These writers include some of "my" prodigies. Readers who resist or even resent prodigious novels may find *Book of Numbers* excessive in its details about an artist's failure and a mathematician's success; in its digressions on mummies and mommies; in its geek wordplay and comic set pieces that include gibbering celebrities at a cocktail party in Palo Alto, pranks perpetrated by start-up boy geniuses, and an absurd political argument with a prince in Dubai. But behind the extravagances here, as in the even more manically prodigious and stylistically hyperwrought *Witz*, there is a caustic earnestness that pushes Cohen to exceed literary conventions of proportion and propriety to represent what he sees as an excess of access.

In both our culture and in the novel, personal information is willingly made public, and accessible to corporations and governments seeking profit and power. Here is Principal speaking, it appears, for the author:

> *We want to see and be watched, to listen and be heard, and even a cave needs to be famous if only among caves, or to the fighters it hides, to the fighters who storm it, if only to itself. Our appetite for secrets is our appetite for fame. How many we keep is how much we lack. Then we divulge around the fire. Then we only have others to live for.*

Autobiographer Cohen and his over-divulging email correspondents represent the first excess of access. Principal's system enables the second, and novelist Cohen throws all their voices into what might be called sacrificial realism, the artist giving up accessible artfulness to imitate contemporary ugliness, the Age of Glut and Gluttony co-terminus with the Digital Age.

An early meaning of "prodigy" was "omen" or "warning." Cohen's premonition is similar to that of the real Julian Assange, in an essay entitled "Google Is Not What It Seems." I worry that *Book of Numbers* may be dismissed as a tardy expose of overreaching corporate power, but Cohen's achievement — and it is substantial as well as inventive — lies in his now ancient (in tech terms) history of Internet search, and his presentation of local moral compromises in Silicon Valley that, like the butterfly wings of the chaos theory discussed in the novel, caused global illegal consequences. The book-producing character Cohen accuses the screen-displaying Cohen of ruining the codex book, but I believe author Cohen finds in the computer and the Internet his models, as well as his subjects, for the density, range, and scope of his systems novel. *Book of Numbers* is the next stage forward of that form. Like Joshua Cohen the mathematician, Joshua Cohen the systems novelist wants to "engineer the ultimate. The connection of connections."

✳✳✳

As I write this summary early in 2017, it's hard to say exactly what will be needed from artists during the Trump administration. I trust there will be inspired farces and brilliant parodies, major Trumpciads and epic satires. But comedy may not be an adequate literary response to uncover the underlying structures of Trumpism. I believe that only the systems novel can place and understand Donald Trump within the historical and economic and media systems that created him. Any one of these three younger novelists, if sufficiently enraged, could produce such a novel. Powers has already published this kind of book in *Gain* with its three components — corporate history, family illness, and the advertising industry. McCarthy's *C* has the historical scope and scientific knowledge I have in mind. Cohen, however, looks to be the most likely candidate. Cohen is my first hope because he has already written for *N + 1* a detailed and disgusted expose of Trump's failed presence in Atlantic City. Cohen also seems to know more about American delusions and deceptions than any of his contemporaries. And I believe he is the writer most capable of the decapitating outrage and artistic excess needed for the novel to have a substantial effect in Trump time. But maybe some new prodigy will emerge to create a prodigious fiction as profound, comprehensive, innovative, and scarified as *Gravity's Rainbow* or *The Public Burning*, two grand and grandiose systems novels of the last century that I hope will be models of literary response for novelists in this century.

THE ONLY BOOK YOU'LL EVER NEED

Before using this title, I Googled it. Many books made this claim in their titles or subtitles. Books about runes and herbs and investments and guitars and numerous other subjects. But none in the first 50 entries about politics or whales. Wait. New e-book software allows me to see your hand moving to click away from this page. I know you. After teaching literature for 40 years, I know your objections to and resentments of *Moby-Dick*, your feeling that, in Ahab's word, it "heaps" you, assaults and maybe even insults you with its mass and information, "insults" because it makes you know more than you thought you ever wanted to know about the "watery part of the world." Wait now, because I'm about to make it easy on you. No, not to offer one of those humorous "Trump Book Reports" circulating on Twitter, but to say that if you don't have time to read the books and writers I've recommended you can read *Moby-Dick*, a grand synthesis of the themes and forms discussed in previous essays.

Melville's book, published in 1851 when whales were being harpooned so Americans could read at night, is an environmental novel for what I've called "Trump's 'Age of Lead.'" Like Coover's *The Public Burning*, *Moby-Dick* is an epic, a democratic book of multiple American voices, ethnicities, and races. It is, like *The Iliad*, a tragedy with a protagonist who has regressed to a pre-literate obsession with honor and fate. *Moby-Dick* is also a "systems novel," probably the first in America, for Melville refers in his

"Cetology" chapters about whales and whaling to sciences and technologies, as well as humanistic disciplines, that demonstrate the planetary complexity that his monomaniacal protagonist would ignore or destroy in his quest for power.

For you — for us — *Moby-Dick* is a comprehensive early warning, a literary response to usurpation, a profound political novel that brings together all these elements — epic and tragedy, ecology and other ologies — in its story of a ship, the *Pequod*, sailed to destruction by a tyrant, Ahab, who makes false promises to and emotionally manipulates his sailors in order to avenge what he sees as an insult to his person, his humiliation by the white whale. As he tells first mate Starbuck, "I'd strike the sun if it insulted me." A whaler named for an Indian tribe, the *Pequod* is also the American ship of state, manned by Indians, blacks, immigrants, and native-born whites — the officers who attempt to check and balance the authoritarian executive, Ahab. But like Coover's Uncle Sam and America's Donald Trump, "magnetic" Ahab exploits the passions of the uneducated crew — for profit, for excitement — to prove his mastery and aggrandize himself. To help control his mates and harpooners, Christian Ahab brings aboard and conspires with Fedallah, a mysterious dark advisor associated with Satan and, for Starbuck, with evil. As the voyage goes on, Ahab alienates other captains he meets, distances himself in royal solitude from the crew, and leaves behind technical aids, such as the log and line, that would detract from the satisfaction of his egocentric mission. Mutiny is impossible, Starbuck decides against assassination, Ahab rages on. Maybe even Donald Trump, the non-reader, knows what happens in the end since the story has been filmed several times: Ahab is killed by Moby Dick, he destroys the *Pequod*, and Ishmael alone survives to tell the tale.

What my sketch of plot and protagonist leaves out are the novel's psychological drama and the emotions it elicits from those readers who reach the book's second half. In a remarkable admission, Donald Trump has said, "I don't like to analyze myself because I might not like what I see." In Ahab's late colloquies with Starbuck and in Ahab's soliloquies, you will find the closest literary approximation I know of the psychological interior that I believe Trump fears to investigate: the feelings of a narcissist struggling to believe in his narcissism by imposing it on everyone else. Ahab "has been in colleges, as well as among the cannibals." He has linguistic and conceptual capabilities that Achilles couldn't imagine and that Trump lacks, but Ahab's wrath is similar to that of the Greek demigod insulted and angered by the loss of a female slave. Achilles, Ahab, Trump — they are a triumvirate of men driven by pre-literate honor.

Ahab has suffered literal injury, losing a leg to Moby Dick. But, like the archaic Greek, Ahab sees the whale — not as Starbuck's "dumb brute" — but as an agent of the gods. For Ahab, the personal becomes the cosmic, and the college man becomes the paranoid male because his body and ego have suffered a primal wound, his "dismasting" a symbolic castration for Melville. Unhappy on land with his wife, Ahab goes to sea to seek revenge and wreak his power on nature. There are no women on the *Pequod*. Around Trump there are always women upon whom he can inflict his narcissism and assert his dominance through sexual bragging, voyeurism, insult, assault, and asymmetrical marriage. Ahab is the villain of *Moby-Dick*. But as many commentators have said, Ahab is the novel's secret hero because, in Melville's words about Hawthorne, Ahab says "No! in thunder" to the Christian God with whom Melville was in a lifelong battle. Secular readers empathize with Ahab's theological rebellion, and readers of *Moby-Dick* may well develop sympathy for Donald Trump as a man fearful of the unconscious that appears to demand he assert his power in every possible way. I would not be surprised to learn, if I can outlive my coeval and read biographers who no longer fear his wrath, that Trump suffered some sexual "wound" as a youth, some shameful failure or wooden leg experience that he has spent his whole life repressing and compensating for. My speculation is not a reason to read *Moby-Dick*. Read it to learn how even in the mid-nineteenth century, an age possibly more literate than our own, the pre-literate psyche can produce tragedy, can destroy a ship and community under its rule.

When discussing *Moby-Dick* with university students, my toughest sell was its Cetology, a word I believe Melville made up from the Latin for whale: *cetus*. Melville had to provide his landlubbers with information about a whaling ship and the whales it pursued to give ballast to his philosophical and religious meditations, and to prepare readers for plot developments. Of course we need to know the biology of the whale. But we also have chapters about the whale in zoology, geology, and archaeology, in sacred texts, in history, in literature, in visual art, in the sea and on land, alive and dead. We have the sociology of whales. We learn about the parts of the whale, its head and its tail, its very large penis, and we learn about the technologies that allow men to cut the whale into its constituent parts, to turn living substance into a commodity, to liquidate life. In short, we learn the systems of the whale and the systems used to process the whale. Melville's seeming excess of information is the device that draws our attention to *Moby-Dick* as an early systems novel, an environmental fiction from which there are many direct lines to that great eco-fiction of the last century, *Gravity's Rainbow*, including the line from whale oil to motor oil, the depths of nature transformed for man's profit and convenience. Throughout *Moby-Dick* Melville plays with lines and circles, with the linear most often associated with the death plot of Ahab, the circular associated with the living interrelations of nature. The man who says "'all visible objects…are but pasteboard masks'" that humans must "'strike through'" dies roped with a harpoon line to Moby Dick. The *Pequod* disappears under the waves, nature wins, the sea rolls on, but we now know Ahab's imperial attitude toward nature is responsible for threatening whales with extinction. Melville's was the Age of Oil, precursor to our Age of Lead.

As a systems novel, *Moby-Dick* has much to teach us about the role of human hubris in planetary ecology, but the novel may be even more important for its epistemological ecology. The novel's subtitle is "The Whale." Only one vowel separates "whale" from "whole," and Melville wanted to get as close as he could to "comprehension," in both its meanings. If you can see Melville's Cetology as standing for the multiple ways we know any subject, you will appreciate *Moby-Dick* as a remarkable early example of intellectual pluralism, a book with enormous respect for science and fact but also a book that knows there can be multiple interpretations of facts. What does this have to do with Trump you may ask. Unlike Trump, Melville was a reader, an adventurer on the sea and in books, an autodidact who read widely and somewhat indiscriminately. This open- and large-minded man was often an economic failure because he wanted to spend his time reading, thinking, and writing.

Like his creator, schoolmaster Ishmael is a literal and figurative reader, a curious perceiver and cautious interpreter — of the tattoos on his friend Queequeg's body, of the lines on a whale's forehead, of the furrows in Ahab's brow, and, most significantly, of the patterns on a gold doubloon that Ahab nails to a mast, an incentive and reward for the man who sights Moby Dick. After Ishmael describes the doubloon, Ahab has this to say of the images on the coin:

> *There's something ever egotistical in mountain-tops and*
> *towers, and all other grand and lofty things; look here,*
> *— three peaks as proud as Lucifer. The firm tower,*
> *that is Ahab; the volcano, that is Ahab; the*
> *courageous, the undaunted, and victorious fowl, that,*
> *too, is Ahab; all are Ahab.*

The novel's other characters approach the doubloon and "read" it in their own personal terms. Ishmael records all their readings, but does not impose a reading himself, nor does he seem particularly interested in the gold, always Trump's goal. Ahab is a monomaniac, and other characters are at least mono-cognitive. Ishmael learns over the course of the long voyage to perceive shipmates — particularly his "other" friend Queequeg, and even Ahab — with objectivity and sympathy. Learned tolerance of others and their strange ideas is why the reader Ishmael survives, bobbing on Queequeg's coffin on the surface of the empty sea.

You may say, "Someone had to survive to narrate the story." Melville could have told the tale, as he says, "omnisciently exhaustive," as most novels were narrated in his era. And at times he forgets that Ishmael is his narrator, but I think Melville insisted on Ishmael's first-person narration as a model of any person's ability to see, like the whale with eyes on either side of its head, contradictory views. The chapter "The Whiteness of the Whale" is the best example, for Ishmael recounts polar (no pun intended) interpretations of the color white. Ishmael is also a model of the ideal reader's literary response to the novel. Ishmael's multiple ways of understanding his experience should be every reader's ways of processing *Moby-Dick* — as well as the complex world it represents and the world of today. Ishmael's survival is a victory of the literate person's open mind, tolerant of others' points of view, not fearful of introspection, slow to decide, not quick to anger. Ishmael is patient in the face of all that he doesn't know.

He does not view difference and mystery as insults, as some impatient readers do when responding to *Moby-Dick*. Here, at a meta-level, is what *Moby-Dick* has to do with Trump. It warns us of the tragedies Trump's pre-literate Ahabism can cause and offers the comedy, the happy ending, of Ishmael's literate and literary mind as a saving alternative to the honor-crazed power of an Ahab or Trump.

Hundreds of books and thousands of essays have been written about *Moby-Dick*, demonstrating the intellectual pluralism of the novel. I'm therefore uncomfortable sucking from such an immense and complex work a few political, moral, and epistemological "lessons" for the Age of Trump — and then using them to claim *Moby-Dick* is the only book you'll ever need. But not so uncomfortable that I don't press *Moby-Dick* on you now that I am no longer able, like an Ahab of the classroom, to force students to read it. *The Public Burning* is indeed closer to our time, is more explicitly about politics, and also has multiple points of view, but in all its satiric wrath it has no Ishmael, no admirable figure to show how an Uncle Sam or an Ahab can be survived, if not defeated. The other novelists I've mentioned as possible fellow travelers with Coover may or may not choose to follow him into satire, epic or not. So we are left to extrapolate from 150 years ago if we want both an attack on monomania and a character who discovers how to resist it.

"Dollars damn me," Melville wrote to Hawthorne when, under his influence, Melville was trying to turn his original adventure tale into the literary novel we now have. Dollars and lawyers put Coover in purgatory when he was trying to publish *The Public Burning*. Both books were courageous and heroic — and received mostly negative reviews. Melville never really recovered, became a customs inspector, and gave up writing fiction for many years. Coover had his university position and continued to write with some success. I mention the authors' histories and circumstances because I believe books that take the time and knowledge displayed in both are newly endangered, not just by the corporate publishing I discussed in "Final Words" but also by the Trump administration's threat to do away with the National Endowments for the Arts and Humanities. They subsidize small, independent presses and give grants to writers (and other artists) to do the research necessary for information-rich books such as Melville's and Coover's. We think of freedom of the press in journalistic terms. The Endowments support the freedom of the presses.

Moby-Dick and *The Public Burning* are massive accumulations of facts. We may not think of the books as "nonfiction novels" such as Capote's *In Cold Blood* or Mailer's *The Executioner's Song*, just to name a couple about murderers. But in fact, Melville and Coover are as respectful of fact as historians. They do not attempt to deny facts or objective truths. When Coover makes Uncle Sam a fly-by-night superhero, we know it's a fiction. When Melville puts Shakespearean language into the mouths of his sailors, we assume it's fictive license. Clearly fictive elements are embedded in and arise out of the authors' research, either on ships or in libraries. The dosey doe of fiction and fact takes place within the context labeled "fiction."

From the Trump administration, we have "alternative facts" disseminated within the context of supposed truth. In that context, Chuck Todd of NBC was correct to label "alternative facts" as "falsehoods." Other journalists called them "lies." In the next four years, we will need intrepid journalists and independent scientists to establish facts and call out falsehoods since the Trump administration in its first few days appears committed to a policy of the big and repeated lie. But we also need novelists to deform some facts — make Uncle Sam fly — and to apply some magic to realism to perform two important functions. Reveal the systems, actual or mythical, beneath the surface of daily facticity and elicit emotional response to characters who struggle to separate knowledge from deception. Given Hillary Clinton's popular vote and the historically low rating for Trump as he begins his residency in the White House, perhaps there will be a robust market for engaged and critical novelists. Philip Roth decades ago remarked on the novelist's difficulty competing with the absurdities of American life. How much more difficult will it be for novelists to compete with a government in the fiction business of alternative realities and "alternative facts" and what Roth has recently called in *The New Yorker* a "river of lies" by the "con man" Trump?

Novelists are like the "Lying Cretan," liars who admit they are liars. Trump is a liar who never admits it and appears to make lying an official, though unstated, policy. We will need writers to dispute him, correct him. And we will need literate readers — like Ishmael — to counter Trump's unscrupulous monomania. Not just literate readers but literary, which is literate on Human Growth Hormone. Literary readers do not think any more carefully than literate people, but literature trains one to care about and care for language as a sensitive instrument, not just a blunt tool for propaganda and power. I'll quote Wittgenstein again: "The limits of my language mean the limits of my world." The world of literature is large with possibilities of imagination and thought and feeling. The world of pre-literate Donald Trump is small, impoverished by ignorance and fear and anger. Literary responses to Trump may not bring down a president or even affect his policies, but literary artists still must continue to provide models of rigorous thought and rich expression — just as medieval monks preserved manuscripts in an earlier dark time — for great and great-minded literature is in and of itself a harpoon, a weapon against the fake "great" and small-minded demagoguery.

EPILOGUE: THE TRUMP LAND

I occasionally return to Trump Tower because I enjoy experimenting with signs, I like to gauge the public's interest in protest, and social contact with Trump supporters keeps my outrage at a useful level. Angered by the proposed repeal of Obamacare, I made a sign with a hole in it. The words said, "TRUMP'S HEALTH CARE PLAN" and an arrow pointed to the hole. The tepid response reminded me yet again the limits of subtlety. When I thrust my hand *through* the hole with my middle finger raised, a lot more people took photos, though no one wanted to talk about insurance. That was the day the reader of fake books on New York City subways showed up to film a few seconds with some button sellers and me. You can watch him reading "Eat, Pray, Grab Pussy" and see my middle finger at *https://www.yahoo.com/news/ comedian-trolls-subway-riders-jaw-153915237.html.* I suppose I should be thankful for my few seconds on an amusing viral tape, and I did have to be there on the street to be filmed, but being a bit player in another person's comedy routine made me wonder yet again about the usefulness of solitary street protest.

My Martin Luther King Day message — "KING'S DREAM: WE. TRUMP'S DREAM: ME, ME, ME" — got me a tip of the hat from a blue jacketed black man and got me embroiled in an argument with a white man over "service." Like many another Trump supporter, he claimed to have served in the military and believed that his protection of America in the past gave him the right to question my patriotism. I thought of Milton's "They also serve who only stand and wait" and pointed out to the veteran that I was standing and serving now, trying to protect him and all the other Trump voters by giving them early warning of Trump's self-aggrandizing deceptions. Another much younger Trump supporter wanted to argue about "we" and "me." When he said, "Half the people in the Midwest are addicted to opioids" I asked the question I always put to Trumpeteers to see if we have any common base of information for further discussion: "Do you read a newspaper?" "No," he said, "the newspapers are all owned by the same five people." I asked my usual second question to gauge my interlocutor's level of literacy: "Do you know the meaning of `hyperbole'?" "What are you," he said, "some kind of grammar Nazi?" "A diction dictator," I told him. He walked away before I could tell him about Walter Ong and the limitations of orality.

When Trump does or says something "unpresidented" or when one of his appointees says something irresponsible or when I see how Americans will suffer from his regressive policies, my outrage spikes and I want to write a new sign: "BROADWAY HISTORICAL HIT AFTER HAMILTON: JOHN WILKES BOOTH." It wouldn't be a threat but a warning, like that sign referring to Huey Long and George Wallace that I first considered. The pre-literate Trump might not understand my sign, but the Secret Service or his intelligence agencies could explain what sometimes happens to demagogues. The message could be mistaken for unliterary hate speech, so I haven't put it on cardboard. I just use my attraction to the idea to gauge my level of outrage that our nation has been hi-jacked by a dangerous dunce. I'm no less enraged than I was when I began making signs. But I want to encourage, so here compacted into three lines is a sign with an allusion to *Gravity's Rainbow*, with Alexander Pope rhymes, and some hip hop doggerel from the base of Trump Tower:

NEVER COWER

BEFORE THE TOWER

OF FAKE POWER.

Before my wife headed to the Women's March on D.C. on January 21st, she went to a sign painting session. She came home carrying one with a yellow background, one with a red, shaming my brown cardboard and magic marker. She said the organizers of the March and the session advised focusing on defending rights, not insulting Trump, so I gave her "HUMAN RIGHTS YES, RITES OF HATE NO." The no insult policy would have constrained my imagination. But that's not the reason I didn't go to Washington. To be honest, I don't want the sign I write to be one in the crowd or my voice lost in the mass chants. That refusal, I suppose, characterizes the literary response. A book is a unique set of self-conscious signs made by one person and best read by another person in privacy and silence. Only such a set of signs that is deeply informed and ingeniously original will have the power of a crowd, will be able to draw to itself a crowd of readers. I have no illusion that *Harpooning Donald Trump* is such a book. I live near a firehouse. First I see the speeding red car with siren wailing. Then come the huge trucks with their frightening blat to clear the way. My hope is to be the red car announcing the heavy literary equipment to come.

I'm happy to report that the British novelist Howard Jacobson has answered my call — before the call was published! — to write what he says is a "savage satire" of Donald Trump in a 50,000-word "fairy tale" entitled *Pussy*, to be published in England in April. According to a report in *The Guardian*, the novella tells the "story of Prince Fracassus, heir to the Duchy of Origen, famed for its golden-gated skyscrapers and casinos, who passes his

99

boyhood watching reality TV shows and fantasizing about sex workers. Idle, boastful and thin-skinned as well as ignorant and egotistical, Fracassus seems the last person capable of leading his country." *Pussy* doesn't sound like "heavy literary equipment," but given the litigiousness of Trump, the fairy tale or fantasy — rather than documentary fiction — is the safe way to beard the beast.

I've written my own tall tale, a sequel to Coover's *The Public Burning*, in the voice of that angry old white man Uncle Sam who regrets advising that angry old white man Trump to run an angry campaign because Sam has to perform the duty Coover assigned him. To "Incarnate" himself in each new president, including Donald Trump, Sam has to sodomize — harpoon — the president-elect to teach him how to "fuck the American public in the ass." My fantasy about a fictional character and a fiction-producing character doesn't really fit in a collection of "A Novelist's Essays," but I'm including "Uncle Sam and Donald Trump" as an appendix. The physiological appendix, I found, is defined as "part of the colorectal anatomy of a human that supports the immune system," so my rectal tale is in the right place. Maybe it will help readers develop immunity to the ass it's about.

On Friday, January 20, I went to Trump Tower with an all-black piece of cardboard that I could flip over for puzzled passersby: "BLACK FRIDAY, BLOCK HATE." The last word I printed in fire car red. It was a bleak day, cold and threatening to rain. But there were more protesters on "my" side of the street — outside the cage! — than I'd ever seen. The blue jackets allowed a group of 20 carrying some professionally made anti-Fascism signs to stand for an hour and be led in chants by a man wielding a loudspeaker! Television cameras in front of the group were blocking pedestrian traffic. What did this relaxation of the rules mean? Had Trump seen the size of his crowd at the inaugural and refused to take the oath? Two women unfurled a large banner over a huge flag pledging no allegiance to hate. They were blocking the Prada windows! Why aren't the blue jackets making them move? A man propped up against a planter three large slabs of cardboard with small print that nobody could read. Last month not even Moses would have been allowed to set down tablets on Fifth Avenue! Nervous newcomers paced back and forth holding their hand-made clichés, unaware that the rules requiring motion were suspended. I was allowed to stay in my choice photo-op spot! I stood alone in silent dignity with my black hole sign. Two blue jackets who knew me came over to shake hands, and one said, "You've been here every day, and these newbies show up today to grab all the attention." They were smiling. I had to laugh and nod because the blues recognized that I wasn't there with Trump Tower at my back just to disseminate the messages on my signs but also to present the example of myself — the persistent solitary protester, a literary figure like Heller's Yossarian and Kesey's McMurphy, heroes of my youth. Here are the ironies: in my weeks of protest very few passersby showed signs of recognizing me as a regular, and most of them were Trump supporters out to heckle. Though I wanted to make a wide impression with my presence, I may have succeeded best with a very narrow and unlikely group — the blue jackets who, I now have reason to believe, could have been saying to them-selves, "Jesus, that old guy is serious. Maybe we should think more about those signs."

Despite being largely ignored and despite the blue jacket's comment, I was happy to see all the protesters, even though some seemed like late partygoers to this angry early bird. An academic friend dropped by to talk with me and suggest an essay on Durkheim's "collective effervescence" and Canetti's *Crowds and Power*. It felt good to be back where this book started, maybe because I knew I'd go home and write its ending. Passersby who did approach me asked if my black sign was mourning. It was,

I told them, but also a warning of darkness falling. Through these days I've been listening to Leonard Cohen's final words in *You Want It Darker*. In the late afternoon on gray Fifth Avenue across from the glitter of Tiffany, the coming months and years looked very dark to me. I had not listened to Trump's "darkling plain" inaugural speech, but I envisioned a dark state consolidating power behind the ignorant orange figurehead. Inauguration day felt like the film *Independence Day* — not a new alien force descending but an old American force of racism, violence, and greed ascending.

To this "darkness visible," as Milton described hell, the literary response will have to be heroic, not just satiric or systemic. Perhaps even a young Pynchon would be too jokey. We may need a Melville or a Whitman, a Faulkner or an Eliot. In my "Introduction" and "Final Words," I said I'd felt like Prufrock and Gerontion before the election.

On January 20th, I felt like Tiresias — "I, Tiresias, old man with wrinkled dugs" in "The Waste Land" — that mythical figure who can see backwards and forwards, the Obama past and the Trump future. But Tiresias could speak only the lines Eliot gave him. Even in The Trump Land I had the freedom to return to Brooklyn and write these lines. The sentiment here is pessimistic, but I'd ask you to see in the dark that literary response is solace and defiance and hopeful. The almost final words of Eliot's poem are "These fragments I have shored against my ruin." The final words of *Harpooning Donald Trump* are

IMAGINATION TRUMPS HATE

-end-

APPENDIX

Uncle Sam and Donald Trump

You don't know about me unless you have read a book by the name of *The Public Burning* by Robert Coover. You know my picture from all those wanted posters, the tall hat with the star, the red bow tie, the blue frock coat, that puny straggle of a beard, the finger pointing out at you, the bellicose stare of an angry old white man. That Coover gave me a long past, all the way back to America's beginnings. I was a slick-talking con man feeling young and randy, an American superhero flying around in the 50s fighting Commies and frying spies. I'm a lot older now with an artificial hip and aching prostate that hinders my duty to Incarnate myself in each new president. But I'm still an angry white man, so when Donald Trump telephoned I took his call.

At the time he was playing the insult comedian in those large-field Republican debate shows. I told him to get out on the road and be me, be himself, an angry old white man and recruiter of fighting folks. He resisted at first because he thinks he's not old. I told him it was the "old" that made anger authentic because every old white man is angry, not just because he's fat and flaccid like Donald or skinny and stunted like me but because he's lost ground to the coloreds and women and tinted foreigners. "Point your finger at the laggards who aren't cheering you, the journalists who are mocking you," I told him, "scowl and shake your fist, pump up all those angry younger white men and women, rally them `round the flag. Tell `em we're in a war, enemies everywhere."

After my advice started raising his poll numbers, Donald asked me to sign on with the campaign and join him on stage to lend some historical gravitas. He was angry all right, but he was just about the dumbest white man to ever run for president, and I didn't want to get too close. Also I'm not as spry as I was in the 50s and don't like to travel. Young people in airports think I'm with the circus. Older people who got drafted tell me, "We don't want you." And what they call "people of color" say, "I know you don't be wanting me, so go along." Here in New York City, people mistake me for a cast member of *Hamilton* and let me be. I did agree to be an invisible advisor. We talked on the phone almost every day, and I used to come in the back door of Trump Tower for middle of the night "conflabs," as he put it.

I found out some things those first nights not many people know. Donald sleeps only four or five hours because he's not fucking Melania any longer.

"I need to keep up my energy for campaigning. It's better than sex. It's like a ten-thousand-some. All those red-faced white folks breathing hard and screaming with joy. You know that red cap I wear? I started using it to keep my comb back in place. But people see it as the red head of my big dick. They see me as a giant dick. Forgot about the hands. It's the head people want, and I give it to them."

"How does Melania feel about this?"

"Melania? She doesn't want to ball an old man with a flabby belly, and I can't wear my corset in the sack. She needs her beauty rest, she says, and that's fine with me because she has to look young and beautiful to remind voters I'm young and bountiful in my red cap. What happens after the election I don't know. I might have to move to Russia. They have a lot of young white women over there."

By the way, I'm editing Donald here, not adding anything, just putting a little order into his jumbled, jumbo sentences. Coover called me unreliable, but I'm too old to be screwing around much with another person's words. At my age, I have enough trouble remembering the ones I want to use, though there's no problem keeping ahead of the "giant dick" in the diction department.

After a few of those late nights, Donald asked, "Is it really true about the Incarnation?"

He knew it was. It's general knowledge in Washington, and there are plenty of living former presidents he could have consulted. The Incarnation is not a job I like, but sodomizing new presidents is how they're prepared to fuck the American public in the ass. I've planted the flag in every president except Obama. I just couldn't bring myself to fuck a black man, and that's probably why he wasn't an angry man for eight years. Since Donald didn't ask me about the Incarnation right away, I figured he was evading something. Later on, after he won, I found out he was hiding something.

"I thought the Intarnation,"[sic] Donald said, "was, you know, just like something that wasn't literally true but, this is what I thought, believe me, like a hyperbole, maybe like a lie, you know some kind of, what do you call it, politic license."

That's Donald uncut, so you can see why I've done a little editing. It's hard to listen to him stumble around, even more unpleasant to read his fumbling.

"It's the truth, Donald. Uncle Sam is not a post-truth guy. We'd have no Army if he were. Do you want to be president or not?"

"I don't want that bitch to beat me. That's what I want most, to beat that bitch who thinks she's smarter than all my wives put together just because she's old and ugly."

That pissed me off some because I'm old and ugly and so is Donald, though he has bought himself some young hair and skin coloring, probably the only candidate except Obama who doesn't want to look snow white. Donald's a grandpa, and former presidents ask me why I don't go by "Pop Sam" nowadays. I look the part since I've grown a full beard, cut my hair back to a grizzled butch, have an even scrawnier neck, and wear wire frame bifocals. But I like to remain avuncular because it's rogue uncles, not grandfathers, who have a reputation as dangerous butt-fuckers. "Pop Sam" has too many ambiguities, as if I were an invention of popular culture and not the man responsible for showing presidents how to fuck the public with no chance of bringing new life to the land. Donald says he has a good bit of experience fucking the public with his casinos and hotels and overpriced golf courses, and I just laugh at my boy Donnie and tell him he needs to be ready to fuck all of the United States and plenty of other nations too.

I assured Donald he wouldn't have to buy any KY until the night he was elected, if he was elected. That was months away. Since Donald doesn't worry about any future exceeding a week or so, depending on his golf dates, he slipped the Incarnation out of his mind.

But you've seen the look on his face the morning he visited Obama in the oval office, the way he spread his knees and dandled his head. Like I said, I'm older than I was 70 years ago, so it took some time for me to give Donald the presidential juice. But he had beaten the bitch, and he wanted the power to "royally fuck," he said, all his thousands of enemies, so he lay there on his king size bed and let me put the wood, the woody as the kids used to say, to him. It was no "wham bam, thank you Sam." More like "no fun, when you done?" I told him the wood was good for his prostate, and he said he had a Russian pianist with delicate fingers to massage that for him. Like most angry men, Donald had a puckered asshole, but I was still slow to deliver my presidential gift. He was the oldest man I'd ever had to Incarnate, and there was no pleasure in harpooning him.

One thing I realized while hammering away at Donald's fat ass: I'd seen other presidential dicks, but I never got a glimpse of Donald's because he was lying face down when he summoned me, and he remained prone until I left. Given all his boasting about his big dick, I figured his equipment was undersized, but he was careful not to reveal that secret. In any event, this is kind of a long way around to explain why Donald looked tired and disoriented and humbled — basically fucked out — when he visited the oval office.

He did manage to mumble out a few gracious words somebody probably wrote for him, and he told me later he'd managed to pull Obama aside to ask him how he avoided me.

"Ha," Obama said, "I'm too fast and too cool for that old white motherfucker to punk me. You should have run while you could still run."

I'm getting ahead of myself here. I'm used to being direct, not telling stories. But I don't want any fake suspense about the Incarnation interfering with the real story, which is how I made Donald's campaign. I'd written some angry old white man freelance pieces for Stephen Bannon at *Breitbart News* — "Uncle Sam Is No Sambo." "Sam Proves He's Not Circumcised." That one had a photo of another person's dick, not erect but it looked younger and healthier than mine. "Uncle Sam Is Not Gay. He Does It For The Country." Bannon brought me in to see if I would join the staff at *BN*. I told Bannon I was surprised he wasn't an old man.

He said, "I'm an old soul. I really belong in the early nineteenth century, before the slaves were emancipated and white people were thrown under the bus."

"Wagon wheels," I said.

"What?"

"No buses in 1863. Trains yes, but no buses. If you'd fucked Lincoln, you'd know this kind of thing."

"He's probably the only white man I wish I'd had a chance to fuck. What was it like?"

"Abe was telling me a story about a young boy that got his pecker in the wrong hole and wouldn't finish until I did. He was Dishonest Abe, because after I finished he wouldn't. He just cackled and said he hoped I'd get a chance to do the same someday to Stephen A. Douglas."

Bannon asked if I could write stories that weren't about Uncle Sam, I told him being Uncle Sam is about the only thing I know, and we agreed I'd continue to do freelance work when the anger moved me. He did show me around the office and introduced me to some of his staff. I couldn't believe how many young white men a middle-aged man like Bannon could recruit to join his army of white power.

It was not long after that interview when Trump contacted me. He got my number from Rudy Giuliani, who had paid me large sums three or four times to give him the presidential treatment. He hoped some pre-Incarnations would give him a chance to compete for the real thing. I've seen some big assholes in my day, but Rudy was the biggest, and I had to wonder if he'd been paying others to pretend they were Uncle Sam.

Trump the Deal Maker thought he could make me an offer I couldn't refuse. "Look," he said, "if you join the campaign and I'm elected, it will be all old angry white men in the Cabinet. You'll fit right in. We'll make up a new agency, something like `Secretary of American History' or `Director of Recruiting.' You won't have to sit next to that doctor, what's his name, the black guy who talked low when he should have been screaming. BinCarson, something like that."

"I can't lose my non-partisan identity," I told Donald, "and I don't want to overexpose my brand. Companies are already using my image to sell pizza and auto parts."

"No such thing as overexposure," he said. "I'd expose my ass in Times Square if I was paid enough. It's just too bad you don't have a powerful name like mine to work with. Something like Samson."

Donald used all his famous deal-making tricks on me, but I wouldn't budge. Finally, I said, "no deal, but I know just the guy who can help you out, that Bannon who runs *Breitbart*. Bring him in house, and you and I can consult in New York when needed."

That's how Bannon came into the campaign and how he and I got Trump into the White House. Though not old himself, Bannon knew all the obvious angry old white man buttons to push and he knew about displacement. I don't mean the displacement of refugees, though he tarred them as angry young dark men, but symbolic displacement. The abandoned hulks of Rust Belt factories, America's decrepit bridges and exhausted highways, the burned out ghetto high rises, the defunct coal mines — all were symbols of old white men, and only an old white man could be sufficiently angry to revitalize an aged America, turn back the clock to the country's great white youth. Bannon saw the paradoxical appeal of old man Bernie to American youths, but Bannon knew he had a better candidate, one who wasn't Jewish, one who didn't bore with policy, and one who harbored and could project a personal rage, not some class or ideological anger, but a deep and mysterious, possibly even to the candidate, wrath that could be called up on the trail again and again until it became habitual, as constant as the image of Uncle Sam on my poster. Trump didn't just "want" voters. He threatened those who didn't want him. The media didn't want Donald, so they became the enemies at his rallies, the people he pointed his righteous finger at, surrogates for any among the crowd or watching on TV who might not want Donald to be their lord and savior.

After his poll numbers started to climb under Bannon, Donald invited me to a late dinner at the Tower to thank me for recommending Stephen. I accepted his thanks, but also told him he should be a bit wary of Bannon.

"Bannon's not just displaced from the early nineteenth century," I said, "he'd be most at home in the time before Luther."

"Lex Luthor?" Donald asked.

"Martin Luther, the Protestant Reformation."

"I thought it was the Jews who were reformed. Great guys, great lawyers, my son in law belongs to that tribe, and I think the Hebes will go strong for me in the election."

"Bannon is an angry old Catholic under that beard and disheveled look," I told Donald. "If he tries to bring in the Pope as an angry old white man who supports you, just draw the line. "

The election was as tight as that pursed-mouth Jimmy Carter's asshole. The pussy-grabbing tape, the old angry white man's prerogative, came out, but a rumored n-word tape is still in some safe, probably waiting for the highest bidder. Those high-school educated angry white men in the Midwest knew better than to elect an old angry white woman and so tipped their states from blue to red. And a surprising number of white women, maybe disgusted with their depressed husbands, voted for Mr. Red Cap the giant dick.

The first few days after his inauguration, Donald was signing a bunch of old angry white man executive orders to reverse the young cool black man's accomplishments. Donald was starting to govern, beginning to fuck Americans. But he wasn't doing it presidentially. He was still being Uncle Sam, still pointing his finger at the media, shaking his fist at the CIA, ranting on Twitter, threatening private citizens, saying he wanted to fuck all those people who didn't show up for his inauguration. I heard he was quoting me in meetings, "I Want You" to do this, "I Want You" do that. He was even starting to use the third person: "Donald Trump Wants You" to end Obamacare, to fuck Medicare. That last wasn't part of his campaign. It seemed to me that old Donald was denying he was old, though he'd never need Medicare, not with Ivanka and his profiteering sons to support him if he has to pay the taxes he owes.

I called the White House, the operator took Uncle Sam's message ("**The** Uncle Sam?" she asked, "I loved you in *The Public Burning* movie."), and Donald returned my call. He boasted how he and the Republican Congress were getting a fast start fucking Americans and refugees, bragged about his plans to bring back torture, and went on about the wall that "would be so high those fucking greasers will have to head south or swim to Cuba to escape their shit-hole country."

"Listen, Donald," I wedged in. "I'm calling to ask you not to gut Medicare. I'm on it, and it works pretty well."

"What the fuck, Sam. You're on Medicare? OK, the name `Sam' is no `Trump,' but I always assumed you'd made a fortune off your name. What happened to your residuals? I'm still making money from that TV show. An American icon on Medicare! I can't believe it. I'll have my foundation send you a check and we'll get you off the dole. It wouldn't be good optics if word got out that I was fucking Uncle Sam, though I got to admit that sore-ass morning after the Incarnation I'd have been tempted. Well, not me myself but I'd have sent one of my surrogates."

Short attention span Donald forgot that he'd been forced to disband his fraud foundation, so I said, "Don't send money, Donald. Just ease up on Medicare. And one other thing. You know I appreciate your imitation of me. It's much better than Alec Baldwin's imitation of you. But I think now is the time to tone down a little that angry old white man role. It works better out on the trail than in the White House."

"I know, I know. Even Bannon is telling me that. But I can't keep that anger in now that you taught me to release it. I want you to understand me, you of all people."

It sounded like "I Want You" in Donald's mouth, a presidential decree. "OK," I told him.

"You were an Army recruiter, so you probably know that my family sent me away to a military school when I was young. All male, of course. I hadn't been there long when the oldest boys came around and told me I had to be initiated. I thought they meant something like being blindfolded and eating cold spaghetti they said was worms or maybe joining the older boys in a circle jerk if I could get my young dick to cooperate."

I Want You, skeptical readers, to know all these connected sentences are just the way Donald spoke. Hard to believe, I know, but this and what follows are exactly the way he talked that night on the phone, as if his story was being formulated for 60 years to come out eventually through the fog of his usual speech.

"But the initiation for me — and only me, I found out later, though I never found out why — was to be butt-fucked by the biggest dick among them. I fought and screamed, but they held me down and took off my pants. The kid rammed it in and I screamed some more. Thankfully, my Initiation was over a lot quicker than the Incarnation."

Given the fact that Donald lies about everything and always presents himself as a victim, I didn't know whether to believe him or not. So I responded how I thought Donald wanted me to.

"So you were traumatized and enraged as a kid, and have spent the rest of your life fucking women to prove you're a man, not a punk?"

"Something like that I guess, but there's more to it. Getting fucked in the ass was painful at first, but I have to confess that I got to like it. I was the dead center of that boy's attention in a way I've never been when I'm on top doing the fucking. You know, you look down and the woman has her eyes closed or is studying the ceiling."

"I wouldn't know about that Donald. The only people I fuck are presidents."

"Right, I forgot. Anyway, back there in that dorm room I was wanted."

He hesitated to make sure I got his point and, maybe, to uncharacteristically think twice about what he said next.

"So, Uncle Sam, here is what I'm worried about now that I'm on the tip top and have the power to fuck everybody as president. If I liked the attention back then, does that mean the American public will enjoy being fucked in the ass for the next four years?"

It was a question I'd never been asked by earlier presidents. I did my necessary business, planted the power, and they could choose whether or not they wanted to sodomize their citizens. Now Donald feared to do what he really wanted to do because he thought he might cause pleasure instead of pain.

What with the Medicare matter and his boasts and his insults, and maybe because I'm an old--and soon to be a feeble--man with an enlarged prostate, I lied to the liar in chief. "Just about every one of those old white presidents did seem to enjoy it."

"Thanks, Sam," Donald said. "That gives me something to think about, but I'll bet those guys just enjoyed getting the undivided attention of Uncle Sam. I'll see you in four years."

I didn't believe either of Donald's statements was true. One, Donald doesn't "think," not in the way most adults do. He reacts in pain or pleasure as he did when getting banged as a young boy. Two, I doubt I'll be around in four years. Even if I am, my prostate and I won't be getting any erections. And I refuse to Incarnate anyone with my index finger. I'll still be Uncle Sam and angry, but I won't have to stick my dick in some elected asshole any more. I do believe I can live without that, though maybe not without Medicare. Perhaps I'm not really needed any longer. With whites becoming a minority soon in America, there will be plenty of angry white men and women, old and young. They won't be needing an old symbol of old white anger. Donald may also not be around or be electable in four years. All that rage from childhood may blow a hole in his heart or brain. And since he and Bannon are unprepared simpletons, maybe the American public will get up off their bellies and throw them out.

Uncle Sam doesn't know the future, but right now I Want You to know this: I did my best to save your asses, but you have been burned by that angry old con man and now I'm pretty sure you will be fucked whether you like it or not.

— end —

ABOUT THE AUTHOR

Tom LeClair grew up in Plymouth, Vermont, the home-town of Calvin Coolidge. He received a B.A. from Boston College, an M.A. from the University of Vermont, and a Ph.D. in English from Duke University in 1972.

He taught American Literature at the University of Cincinnati from 1970 to 2008, when he retired as Professor of English and Nathaniel Ropes Chair. He moved to Brooklyn in 2008 and held the title "Professor Ping Pong" at SPiN, NYC, from 2009 until his retirement in 2015.

Tom LeClair began writing as a literary critic, publishing *In the Loop* and *The Art of Excess* in the late 1980's before turning to fiction with *Passing Off* (1996), the first of his "Passing" trilogy. Since 1972, he has published hundreds of essays, reviews, stories, and interviews in nationally circulated periodicals. Some of those works were collected in *What to Read (and Not)*. He has published three other novels in addition to the "Passing" sequence.

Awarded a Fulbright Professorship at the University of Athens, Greece, in 1981-82, LeClair has lived in Greece about a quarter of the time since then. He was a fiction judge for the National Book Awards in 2005 and has written an essay about the NBA fiction finalists each year since 2008.

ACKNOWLEDGMENTS

Two essays in *Harpooning Donald Trump* appeared, under different titles, in *The Daily Beast*: "Impressions of a Solitary Protester" and "The Public Burned." The material in "Systems Novelists We Need Now" originally appeared as reviews in *The Barnes and Noble Review*. Material on lead in "Trump's 'Age of Lead'" was first published in *Full Stop*.

I'd like to thank the old novelists club — Jerome Charyn, Don DeLillo, and Joseph McElroy — for encouraging this project and for visiting me at Trump Tower; Malcolm Jones at *The Daily Beast* for publishing early essays; Charles Blow of *The New York Times* for his persistent and eloquent outrage; Jim Bergman at *Mediacs* for getting this book out quickly; Heather and Wayne Hall, Jim Cummins, Inga Manticas, and Lee Kellogg for commenting on some of the essays; and my wife Annaliki for long underwear and other support during some cold days at Trump Tower.